W9-AFJ-270

OXFORD MEDICAL PUBLICATIONS

Eating disorders

THE FACTS

Eating disorders

THE FACTS

SUZANNE ABRAHAM
and
DEREK LLEWELLYN-JONES

*Department of Obstetrics and Gynaecology
Sydney University*

OXFORD NEW YORK TOKYO
OXFORD UNIVERSITY PRESS

RC
552
A5
A37

Oxford University Press, Walton Street, Oxford OX2 6DP

Oxford New York Toronto
Delhi Bombay Calcutta Madras Karachi
Kuala Lumpur Singapore Hong Kong Tokyo
Nairobi Dar es Salaam Cape Town
Melbourne Auckland

and associated companies in
Beirut Berlin Ibadan Nicosia

Oxford is a trade mark of Oxford University Press

© Suzanne Abraham and Derek Llewellyn-Jones, 1984

First published 1984
Reprinted 1985

All rights reserved. No part of this publication may be reproduced,
stored in a retrieval system, or transmitted, in any form or by any means,
electronic, mechanical, photocopying, recording, or otherwise, without
the prior permission of Oxford University Press

British Library Cataloguing in Publication Data

Abraham, Suzanne
Eating disorders.
1. Appetite disorders
I. Title   II. Llewellyn-Jones
616.852   RC552.A72
ISBN 0-19-261459-2

Library of Congress Cataloging in Publication Data
Abraham, Suzanne.
Eating disorders.
Bibliography: p.
Includes index.
1. Anorexia nervosa.   2. Bulimarexia.   3. Obesity.
I. Llewellyn-Jones, Derek.   II. Title. [DNLM:
1. Appetite disorders.   2. Obesity.   WI 143 A159e]
RC552.A5A37 1984   616.85'2   841-782
ISBN 0-19-261459-2
ISBN 0-19261526-2 (Pbk)

Printed in Great Britain by
Richard Clay (The Chaucer Press) Ltd,
Bungay, Suffolk

Acknowledgements

We wish to acknowledge those colleagues who have been involved in the research or who have helped us in the development of this book. They include Professor P.J.V. Beumont, Professor R. Kalucy, Professor Don McNeil, Professor Ian Fraser, Dr Michael Mira, Dr Catherine Mason, Dr Peter Stewart, Dr Warren Argall, Mr Timothy Sowerbutts, Mr V. Gebskie, Toni Chambers, Minnie Donovan, and option term medical students of Sydney University.

We thank our secretaries, Carole Kirkland, Judy Shade, Jeanette Vizzard, and Pamela Wray who uncomplainingly have typed and re-typed drafts of our manuscript; and helped us in other ways. We would also thank the staff of Oxford University Press.

Most of all we thank our patients. Without them there would be no book. We would particularly thank those patients who permitted us to use their letters or tape recordings (appropriately modified for reasons of privacy) for the case histories and quotations.

NOTE

Because of the problems of gender in the English language, we have had to decide whether to use 'he' or 'she' when referring to people. We feel that to use 'person' in each instance is distracting. As we treat more women than men, and as more women than men develop eating disorders, we have chosen to use she rather than he in all instances. The reader should not deduce that we have any sexist bias.

In this book a 'binge' refers to an episode of compulsive over-eating, not a drinking bout. We have used the term as our patients describe their eating behaviour as 'bingeing' or binge-eating.

The nosology of insanity, the etiology,
the symptomatology, pathology, diagnosis,
prognosis, the care — how nicely the
textbooks classified everything! How
accurately they defined the idiot, the
cretin, the imbecile, the epileptic, the
hysteric, hypochondriac, and neurasthenic.
Instead of admitting that little was known
about what went on in the human brain,
either healthy or sick, the professors
stacked up Latin names.

from *The Estate*
Isaac Bashevis Singer

Contents

1

Adolescent eating behaviour

If I was going to get a job when I left school, I felt I had to be half a
stone lighter. All my friends were dieting but my mother disapproved.
She said it was puppy fat which would disappear. I knew it wouldn't,
so I had to pretend I was not hungry because I wanted to be slim.

For most of recorded history a woman was seen as desirable when her
body was plump due to the deposition of fat on her breasts, hips, thighs,
and abdomen. It was fashionable to be fat. The cultural belief that to
be fat was to be attractive was due to the uncertainty of food supplies
in pre-industrial and early industrial societies, to the irregular occurrence
of famines, and to the effects of pandemics which eliminated large
numbers of farm labourers. A curvaceous female body indicated that
the husband (or father) was prudent, efficient, and affluent. It also
indicated that the woman had sufficient energy stored in the form of
food in her larder to protect her family and in the form of fat on her
body to protect herself in times of scarcity.

In the past 75 years, with abundant food supplies and good food
distribution in many of the developed nations of the Western world,
almost for the first time in history slimness has begun to become
fashionable. This is documented in fashion magazines, in records of the
'vital statistics' of women winning beauty contests, and in books about
diet which now appear at least every year. For the past two decades the
public perception has been that a woman is attractive, desirable, and
successful when she is slim. A study of the vital statistics of *Playboy*
centrefolds and of competitors in the finals and the winners of the
Miss America Pageant Contest over the past 20 years shows that, although the preferred breast size has varied, and there has been a slight
increase in the height of the women, their weights have decreased and
are below the average of American women of similar age and height.

Over the same period, articles on 'new and exciting' diets (often
nutritionally inadequate and occasionally dangerous) have appeared at

1

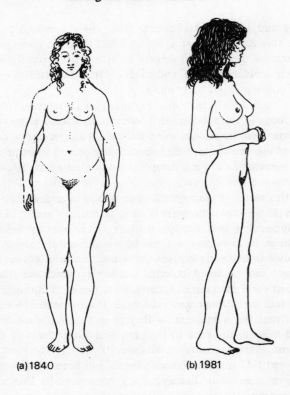

(a) 1840   (b) 1981

Fig. 1. The changing fashion in women's figures. The first illustration is taken from an obstetrical textbook printed in England in 1840, the second from a textbook produced in 1981.

regular intervals in women's magazines, and the number is increasing. The publication of 'new and revolutionary' diet books is also increasing. Most people living in the developed nations also receive a constant stream of impressions from television commercials which use young, attractive, and lissom women to advertise products as diverse as soft drinks and security investments, cars, cigarettes and computers, fast foods and floor polishers.

The messages from the media stress how desirable it is for women to

2

be young and to be or to become thin. These messages particularly influence teenage women at a period when they are undergoing emotional stress as they seek to achieve independence from their parents, to compete with their peers, and to find their identity. Adolescence is a time of concern about body image.

In late childhood hormonal changes trigger an increase in height in girls and boys. The increase, or growth spurt, occurs at an earlier age in girls than boys and is achieved by the child increasing the amount of food he or she eats. In girls the onset of the growth spurt precedes the onset of menstruation and overlaps its establishment at an average age of 12½ years. There is a wide time range in the onset and duration of the growth spurt and the peak may be reached by girls as early as 10 or as late as 15. The growth spurt is accompanied by marked changes in the bodily appearance of the two sexes, which in turn are dependent on the sex hormones which are now being produced in the girl's ovaries or the boy's testicles. Both sexes show an increase in muscle bulk but this is much more marked in males. Girls have a particularly large spurt in hip growth and, in contrast to boys, do not lose fat during the growth spurt. In fact, girls have a general tendency to increase their body fat, particularly on the upper legs, as they cease to gain height. Fat is also deposited beneath the skin, in the breasts and over the hips. Obviously the amount of fat deposited is related to the energy absorbed from the food the girl eats and is influenced by the hormonal changes which are occurring at this time. Energy intake from food is limited by the person's appetite. During early adolescence, unknown factors stimulate the teenager to eat more, with the consequence that the energy intake for females reaches a maximum during the age range of 11 to 14, at a time when her energy needs are great. From about the age of 14, a teenage girl's energy needs fall, but if she continues to eat the same amount as she has been eating she will absorb an excess of energy which will be converted into fat, and she will become fat. She has to control her food intake, in order to control her weight (Figs. 2 and 3).

This is the adolescent female's dilemma. She may wish to remain thin or to become thin, because cultural norms expect her to be thin, or she may reject those norms, either because of conflict within herself or within her family, or because she enjoys and finds emotional release in eating. If she chooses to become and remain thin, she has to learn

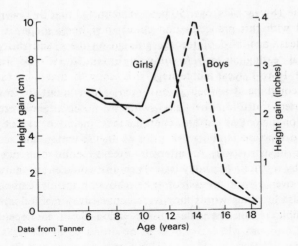

Fig. 2. The 'spurt' in growth at puberty.

new eating habits, because she will inevitably become fat if she continues eating the quantity of food she has become used to eating. Her perception of her body is important to her psychological well-being. She may see her body as large and overweight compared with those of fashionable and popular media personalities. It is significant that, in contrast to older women, adolescent girls perceive their bodies part by part, noting particularly the size and shape of their breasts and the size of their thighs, bottom, hips, and abdomen. The thighs are particularly vulnerable to an overperception of size – the girl perceiving her thighs as larger and uglier than they usually are.

The overperception of body size is found amongst teenage girls in many countries. A study of 1000 teenagers attending high schools in the United States showed that the girls were particularly preoccupied with their body shape and their weight. About half of them classified themselves as obese, although anthropometric measurements showed that only 25 per cent were obese by the criteria used by the authors, which were based on standard United States weight, height, and age tables. In a Swedish study of the entire female population of a small town, 26 per cent of 14 year olds perceived themselves as fat; and among the 18-year-olds, over 50 per cent reported that they were fat.

Faced with this preoccupation about their body shape, it appears that at least one-third of teenage girls go on diets, and many go on occasional 'eating binges'. A study in Britain in 1976 of the eating habits of 16-to-17-year-old teenage girls, showed that their eating behaviour could be described as disturbed. The amount of food eaten daily varied fourfold. The daily swings of food intake were superimposed on a monthly pattern. Energy intake, mainly of carbohydrates, tended to increase in the week prior to menstruation and to decline following menstruation. At intervals after a period of strict dieting (usually by restricting carbohydrates) the girls would eat large quantities of food over a short period of time, choosing mainly carbohydrate-rich foods. In other words they were compulsive or binge-eaters. It is not possible to use these data to generalise about adolescent eating

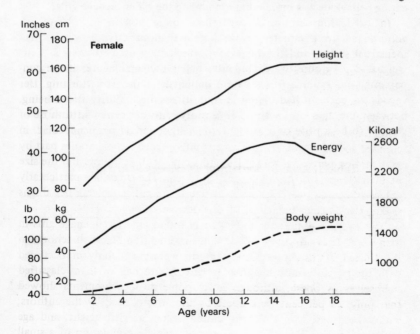

Fig. 3. Energy intake and growth of adolescents.

behaviour in other countries; this pattern of eating may have been peculiar to London teenagers at that time.

A study in Sydney made five years later showed that Australian female students aged 18 to 22 decreased their intake of carbohydrate, protein, and fat, and hence of energy, in the premenstrual period but increased their intake in the day or two before and during menstruation. Individual women showed a wide daily variation in food intake, the amount eaten depending on how the women felt. A decreased food intake may result in hunger and craving for food, with the result that when the woman felt better she ate more or even went on an eating binge.

The Sydney study showed that the daily quantity of food eaten would vary fourfold. In the Swedish study, one-third of the teenage girls alternated dieting with periods of compulsive eating, and such eating behaviour was more common among the older teenage girls.

In 1981, four groups of Australian young women aged 16 to 30 volunteered to complete a questionnaire about their eating habits, menstrual status, and the behaviour which they used to control their weight. The groups were students, ballet dancers, anorexia nervosa patients, and bulimia (binge-eater) patients. Of the 106 students surveyed, 94 per cent had dieted at some time, the majority first dieting between the ages of 13 and 18. Seventy-nine per cent said that they wanted to be a little or a lot lighter in weight and 31 per cent said that

Table 1. *Areas of body from which weight loss desired*
(106 healthy women aged 15–25)

	Per cent of women
Thighs	64
Bottom	45
Hips	43
Waist	22
Legs	20
Face	9
All over	9
Breast	6
Arms	6

they had difficulty in controlling their weight. Like the Swedish and American teenagers and young women, most of the Australians wanted to lose weight from their thighs, bottom, hips, and abdomen (Table 1). Sixty-three per cent said that they had episodes of overeating when they 'couldn't stop', in other words, they had episodes of binge-eating, and 18 per cent could be described as being binge-eaters. To control their weight, most of the young women avoided eating between meals, took energetic exercise, kept busy to avoid the temptation to eat, missed out one (or more) meals each day, or chose low calorie foods (Table 2). These methods are very similar to those chosen by patients diagnosed as having anorexia nervosa or bulimia. A few occasionally used vomiting as a method of controlling weight, or to relieve the feeling of bloating.

Table 2. *Weight-losing behaviour used by 106 normal healthy women aged 15–25*

	Per cent using
Avoiding eating between meals	78
Exercising alone	75
Dieting ('own' diet)	55
Avoiding eating breakfast	48
Keeping busy to avoid temptation to eat	46
Selecting low-calorie foods	41
Counting calories	34
Avoiding situations where food present	25
'Dieting with a friend'	22
Using illness as an excuse not to eat	21
Exercising with a friend	20
Drinking water before eating	18
'Natural' laxatives	16
Lying about amount of food eaten	16
Weighing self several times daily	15
Smoking cigarettes	14
Following a diet (from a magazine)	12
Keeping the larder empty	12
Avoiding eating with the family and 20 other methods	10

Eating disorders – the facts

The evidence from several Western nations confirms that preoccupation with body shape and size with dietary restriction alternating with episodes of binge-eating, is widespread among female adolescents and young adults. In addition, about one woman in ten induces vomiting periodically as a means of controlling her weight, and a smaller number abuse laxatives for the same purpose.

The cult of acquiring or of maintaining a fashionably slim figure is encouraged by the many articles on dieting and diets in women's magazines and the publication of new best-selling diet books. Their efficiency in helping the reader achieve and maintain a reduced weight is questionable as new diets appear so frequently and disappear as frequently to be superseded by another 'fad' diet. It seems that the twentieth-century female desires a miracle diet which is effective, painless psychologically and physically, and can be adopted with no disturbance to her life-style. No such diet exists or can exist. In spite of a constant barrage of propaganda extolling slim bodies among young people, and in spite of a constant stream of information about diets, the eating behaviour of most adolescent women is under their control and their weight fluctuates within the 'desirable' range for their height and weight. A few young women are unsuccessful in their desire to control their weight, and develop alternating episodes of dieting and over-eating. The loss of control over their eating behaviour results in the development of bulimia, which may disrupt the life of the individual to a considerable degree. Many experience menstrual distrubances, and in some cases the dieting, together with other methods or losing weight, may lead to serious ill health.

Other young women are so concerned about losing control of their eating that they start on a relentless pursuit of thinness. They eat minimal amounts of food, and often use additional methods of losing weight. The result is that they become emaciated and their menstrual periods cease. They develop anorexia nervosa.

Those teenagers who choose to ignore the social pressures to become and to remain thin, and continue eating more energy than they need for their bodily functions, gain weight progressively. In fact a person who is morbidly obese has an energy excess of about 3500 kcal per lb (29 MJ per kg) above the desirable weight; so that she has at least 1300 MJ (300 000 kcal) of excess energy stored as fat.

8

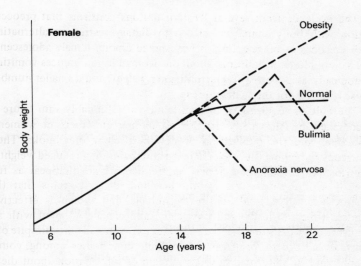

Fig. 4. The onset of eating disorders.

It should be stressed that the eating disorders outlined: anorexia nervosa, bulimia, and obesity (especially morbid obesity) are not *illnesses* in themselves. They become illnesses when they interfere with the person's physical or mental comfort; or disorganize their lives to a marked degree; or so distort their lives that those of close relatives are also disturbed and help is sought. Unfortunately, in severe cases, unless treatment is sought, the eating disorder may lead to the premature death of the victim.

2

Eating disorders

The human being is an open social system, each one, in its own way unique. My food problem is my somewhat unique reaction to a hoard of external and internal influences. Human beings prefer things in a state of organization, they dislike randomness and attempt to classify.

The various eating disorders are more easily discussed if the reader has a clear idea of how they are classified. In this, as in most other psychosomatic conditions, different authorities have slightly different classifications. However we can give a general definition for each disorder by putting together features most commonly described.

ANOREXIA NERVOSA

People may find it hard to believe or comprehend why a person, supposedly intelligent and quite attractive and with a good family upbringing would throw it all away for an obsessive need − no, desire! − to be slender and praised for the will power to diet so well and easily.

The term anorexia nervosa was first used by an English physician, Sir William Gull in 1873. He described a young woman, 'Miss A', whom he had first seen seven years earlier:

Her emaciation was very great. It was stated that she had lost 33 lbs. in weight. She was then 5st. 12 lbs. Height, 5 ft. 5 in. Amenorrhoea for nearly a year. No cough. Respirations throughout chest everywhere normal. Heart sounds normal. Resp. 12; pulse, 56. No vomiting nor diarrhoea. Slight constipation. Complete anorexia for animal food, and almost complete anorexia for everything else. Abdomen shrunk and flat, collapsed. No abnormal pulsations of aorta. Tongue clean. Urine normal. Slight deposit of phosphates on boiling. The condition was one of simple starvation. There was but slight variation in her condition, though observed at intervals of three or four months. . . . The case was regarded as one of simple anorexia.

Eating disorders

Various remedies were prescribed – the preparations of cinchona, the bichloride of mercury, syrup of the iodide of orion, syrup of the phosphate of iron, citrate of quinine and iron, etc., but no perceptible effect followed their administration. The diet also was varied, but without any effect upon the appetite. Occasionally for a day or two the appetite was voracious, but this was very rare and exceptional. The patient complained of no pain, but was restless and active. This was in fact a striking expression of the nervous state, for it seemed hardly possible that a body so wasted could undergo the exercise which seemed agreeable. There was some peevishness of temper, and a feeling of jealousy. No account could be given of the exciting cause. Miss A remained under my observation from January 1866 to March 1868, when she had much improved, and gained weight from 82 to 128 lbs. The improvement from this time continued, and I saw no more of her medically ... The want of appetite is, I believe, due to a morbid mental state. I have not observed in these cases any gastric disorder to which the want of appetite could be referred. I believe, therefore, that its origin is central and not peripheral. That mental states may destroy appetite is notorious, and it will be admitted that young women at the ages named are specially abnoxious to mental perversity. We might call the state hysterical without committing ourselves to the etymological value of the word, or maintaining that the subjects of it have the common symptoms of hysteria. I prefer, however, the more general term, 'nervosa', since the disease occurs in males as well as females, and is probably rather central than peripheral. The importance of discriminating such cases in practice is obvious; otherwise prognosis will be erroneous, and treatment misdirected.

Sir William was in error: anorexia nervosa patients do not have a lack of appetite. They are often hungry, but suppress their hunger and refuse to eat normally, because of their relentless desire to be thin, even to the point of becoming emaciated, and because of their fear that they will lose control of their eating behaviour.

The features of anorexia nervosa are as follows:

1. The woman is abnormally sensitive about being fat, or has a morbid fear of becoming fat, and of losing her control over the amount of food she eats. This fear induces her to adopt behaviour aimed at losing weight. Most anorexia nervosa victims drastically reduce the amount of food they eat, particularly reducing carbohydrate-containing foods (bread, cakes, sweets, sugar) and fatty foods. However, the diet which they choose usually reduces all

11

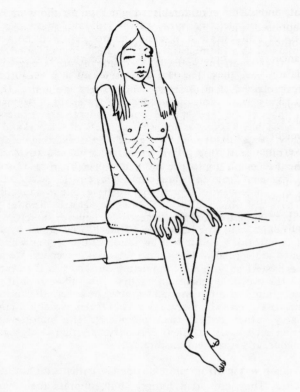

Fig. 5. Anorexia nervosa.

food intake. Some anorexics use other methods of weight-reduction, in addition to limiting the food they eat. The behaviours vary, but self-induced vomiting, the use of excessive amounts of laxatives or diuretics, and strenuous exercise are most common.

2. A woman diagnosed as having anorexia nervosa has lost a considerable amount of weight, so that her weight is usually less than 7 st. (45 kg). An obvious source of diagnostic error could creep in here. For example, women who have severe psychotic mental illness may believe that their food is poisoned, refuse to

eat, and suffer considerable weight loss. Or the woman may be depressed and react by avoiding eating, because she cannot be bothered to eat. Marked physical diseases, such as terminal cancer and tuberculosis, may be associated with extreme emaciation. For these reasons, the woman must have no other physical or psychological illness, which might account for her loss in weight before a diagnosis of anorexia nervosa is made. Once a physical or a mental illness has been excluded, a woman whose weight is less than 7 st. (45 kg) may have anorexia nervosa. However, merely to take a level of weight which makes no allowance for the person's height or age is simplistic, and doctors now tend to use a more sophisticated calculation. Three are used currently. In the first the woman is said to have lost at least 25 per cent of her 'ideal' or 'desirable' body weight, that is the weight which falls into a range of weight for height calculated by insurance

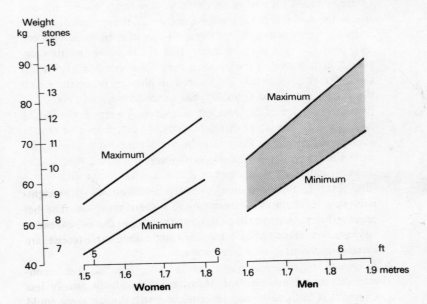

Fig. 6. Maximum and minimum ideal weights for men and women of different heights, wearing indoor clothing.

13

companies (Fig. 6). The second calculation takes into account the person's age, as well as her weight and height, and is called the Average Body Weight (ABW). It is obtained from a table prepared by the Society of Actuaries, which is printed in the Appendix (p. 154). If the woman's weight is less than 80 per cent of the ABW she may have anorexia nervosa.

The third calculation was devised in 1871 by a Belgian astronomer, Dr Quetelet, for diagnosing obesity. We believe it may be of value in reaching a diagnosis of anorexia nervosa. The *Quetelet Index* is calculated from the simple formula W/H^2, that is:

$$\frac{\text{weight in kilograms}}{\text{height in metres} \times \text{height in metres}}$$

The person is weighed in indoor clothing without shoes.

We have calculated the percentage of the ABW and the Quetelet Index for our anorexia nervosa patients and have found the latter to be a more precise measure of the degree of underweight or emaciation. If the person's Quetelet Index is between 19.9 and 15.1 she is underweight and, if the other criteria mentioned in this section are present, may have anorexia nervosa. If the index is 15 or below and she has no physical or mental illness she is emaciated and probably has anorexia nervosa (Fig. 7). A further advantage of the Quetelet Index over Average Body Weight tables is that the latter differ in different countries and change over periods of time. For example, the Metropolitan Life Assurance Company of New York have recently revised their tables upwards as the average weight of Americans has increased.

3. The third feature common to most descriptions of anorexia nervosa is that the woman ceases to menstruate — she becomes amenorrhoeic. Amenorrhoea may occur early in the illness before any great loss of weight has occurred, and menstruation invariably is absent in emaciated women.

These features: a morbid fear of becoming fat; a marked loss of weight (which is not due to any physical or psychological disease), so that the woman weighs less than 80 per cent of her ABW (or has a Quetelet Index of less than 15); and amenorrhoea, establish the diagnosis

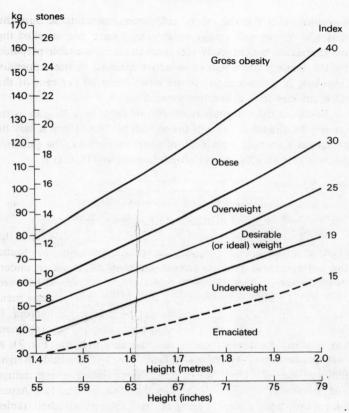

Fig. 7. Weight/height^2 index.

of anorexia nervosa. In addition, a woman suffering from anorexia nervosa may show other psychological or physical disturbances.

It has been claimed that a distorted body-image – the woman perceiving her body as larger, wider, and fatter than it is in reality – is a specific feature of anorexia nervosa. This is inaccurate as many other women, such as pregnant women, who have recently changed their body shape, have the same distorted body-image. It is true that many severely emaciated women suffering from anorexia nervosa lose insight into how emaciated they are, in other words, they deny their thinness.

15

These women have a grossly distorted perception of their body size. But it is also known that many women who have normal eating behaviour overestimate their body size, and in some cases overestimate it considerably more than do women who have anorexia nervosa, especially when looking at their hip width and their body from the side. It is therefore unlikely that a distorted body image is a feature of anorexia nervosa, except perhaps among those who are severely ill.

It is also possible that some of the reports which say that a distorted body image is a specific feature of anorexia nervosa may be due to the patient deceiving the doctor, as in the following case history.

Case history: Clara

I've spoken to other anorexics and they realize just as I realize that at our lowest weights, we all knew we were damn thin. You'd have to be pretty stupid to think that you were not, but you have to hide it because if you let on to the doctors that you know you are thin, they will want to put weight on you. So you keep letting on you don't think you are thin but you think you are normal and they will think your way. I remember two anorexics who were so sincere to the Professor, telling him they were normal. I asked them if they felt like me, falsely sincere and secretive. They said they did. How could they think otherwise with their bones sticking out of their bottoms. The next day when I saw the Professor he said 'Clara, do you think you are thin?' My first reaction was 'see, he doesn't know, he must be dumb. Oh, I won't tell him though, because I want to stay like this: I feel safe, out of the world and men are too scared to touch me in case they break me.' So I answered him 'Of course I'm not thin.'

Women who have anorexia nervosa tend to look at parts of their body, rather than their body as a whole, when they look at themselves in a mirror. They see their abdomen as 'bulgy' and they want it to be flat. They perceive their thighs as ungainly, large, and heavy, and want them to be smooth and thinner. These perceptions also occur to normal women, as we found when we asked several groups of women the question: 'What would you prefer your weight to be?' The groups were of women who were students, ballet dancers, or women with eating disorders. Each of the groups wanted to be thinner (Table 3). When the perceptions of body image by a woman who has anorexia nervosa are further analysed, it becomes apparent that what the woman was saying was that when her weight was normal she saw parts of her body, for

16

Table 3. *What young women would like their weight to be*

	Healthy women (106)	Ballet dancers (50)	Anorexia nervosa patients (22)	Bulimia patients (44)
	Per cent			
A lot heavier	0	1	9	0
A little heavier	1	1	50	0
Present weight	17	3	5	14
A little lighter	47	60	23	18
A lot lighter	32	30	14	64

example her thighs, as too heavy, and although she was now emaciated, she still saw her thighs as heavier and bigger than the rest of her body. In other words, although she knew that she was thin she *felt* that she was fat.

Anorexia nervosa patients have been divided into two groups. The first group, 'the dieters', lose weight by rigorously restricting their food intake (but may have episodes of abusing laxatives). The 'dieters' account for about 60 per cent of all patients. The second group, the 'vomiters and purgers', eat more food (some binge-eating) but prevent it being absorbed by self-induced vomiting and/or the excessive use of purgatives. In this behaviour they resemble many binge-eaters.

BULIMIA, OR BINGE-EATING

Looking back on the reason I started binge-eating, I think it was because of my obsession with dieting. And that stemmed from the fact that I thought I was overweight when in reality I was short and had inherited fatter arms and legs than the average person.

Binge-eaters are the second group of people who have eating disorders. A binge-eater can be described as a person who has a compulsion to eat large quantities of food over a short period of time, usually two hours or less. As in the case of anorexia nervosa, binge-eaters are usually female and the two illnesses have many features in common. However,

17

although 40 per cent of anorexia nervosa patients binge-eat; many binge-eaters do not develop anorexia nervosa. In fact most binge-eaters are of normal weight or are overweight, and at least 10 per cent of obese individuals go on eating binges. These facts have induced the American College of Psychiatrists to differentiate the illness of binge-eating, or compulsive eating, from anorexia nervosa and to give it the name 'bulimia'.

A problem in making the diagnosis of bulimia is that most people binge-eat from time to time. The difference between them and women who have bulimia is that the latter binge-eat frequently (usually more than once a week) and feel that they have lost control over their eating. They have become 'foodaholics'. They divide their days into 'good' days when they have no desire to binge and 'bad' days when the compulsion to binge becomes irresistible. They are aware that anxiety, stress, or unhappiness may precipitate an episode of binge-eating.

Bulimia patients know that they have an eating disorder. They are fascinated by food and buy cookbooks and read magazine articles about food and cooking. They enjoy discussing food and diets, and often use eating as a way of escaping from unpleasant stresses of life, to the extent that they have an all-consuming desire to eat. But they are aware that binge-eating is quite distinct from overeating. Between binges they may diet rigorously, and may try to resist the urge to binge-eat, rather as a dipsomaniac tries to resist the urge to drink. This analogy may be more exact than is obvious at first sight, as at least 20 per cent of bulimia patients abuse alcohol or drugs.

During an eating binge (which usually lasts a few hours but may go on for days) the woman's resistance to eating fails, and she has an irresistible desire to eat. This leads her to ingest excessive amounts of food, far more than she needs to maintain good nutrition and far more than most other people in her culture normally eat. This causes her to be secretive about her binge-eating, at least in the early stages of the illness. She perceives binge-eating as a very private affair, and plans her binges secretively. It may sound bizarre, but in many cases the woman's husband, or partner, or her parents are unaware that she has been binge-eating three or more times a week for a number of years. Many of the women have a safe place where they can binge privately, and where, if they induce vomiting, they can vomit without discovery. When it becomes known by her parents, her partner, or close friends that she binge-eats, attempts to prevent her binge-eating may be met by hostility; or those close to her may condone her behaviour, in the hope that she will stop. As a woman who has bulimia is aware that binge-eating and overeating are distinct, and because she has a fear of putting on weight, she takes measures to make sure that the food she has eaten during an eating binge will not lead to a weight increase. To achieve this she may adopt one or more of several methods. She may diet strictly between eating binges or she may exercise excessively, spending hours each day in the gymnasium, or jogging, playing squash, or swimming. If she finds that these measures do not control her weight, she may resort to a more dangerous method of weight reduction by making sure that the food she eats is not absorbed. She may achieve this by inducing herself to vomit or by taking large amounts of laxatives to make sure that her food is hurried through her gut.

More than half of bulimia patients induce vomiting during and at the end of each eating-binge, and all binge-eaters try to diet between binges, although many fail to keep to their chosen diet. A minority of binge-eaters do not induce vomiting and maintain a very strict diet between eating-binges controlling their weight in this way. Some bulimia patients also abuse laxatives or diuretics between binges in an attempt to keep their weight under control.

There are considerable variations in the weight-losing behaviour of binge-eaters, but, in general, 'vomiters' tend to have a longer history of binge-eating and to take more time in preparing food for the binge. They also seem to have a greater degree of 'feeling good' after a binge, than non-vomiters who are more likely to feel guilty or sad. In other words the feelings of unhappiness, anxiety, or stress which precipitated an eating binge are relieved to a greater extent among those bulimia patients who induce vomiting than among those who use other behaviours to avoid weight gain.

OBESITY

There is considerable controversy among nutritionists as to whether obesity can be classified as an eating disorder. The problem is that people whose weight is 'normal' often eat erratically, sometimes putting on weight, sometimes losing weight. Recently a study was made of over 5000 food choices at various restaurants, snack bars, and cafés. The conclusion of the study was that the major influence on how much people ate was *where* they ate, and that obese people had as wide a range of eating behaviour as 'normal' people. On the other hand many researchers have shown that obese people choose to eat more food and eat it more quickly than non-obese people. Other researchers have argued that obesity, and particularly severe (or morbid) obesity, occurs in people with a psychiatric problem. However, a study of severely obese people in the United States showed that anxiety, depression, low self-esteem, and poor body image reported by severely obese people were a result, rather than a cause, of their obesity. The study added support to the theory that severe obesity is a habitual disturbance of eating. The experience of nutritionists who try to induce severely obese people to lose weight also suggests that obesity is an eating disorder.

The first decision a severely obese person has to make is that she wants to lose weight, either because she finds her body unattractive, or because others remark about her obesity, or because she learns that morbid obesity is dangerous to her health, or that it is aggravating an existing disease such as osteoarthritis or hypertension. The decision to lose weight induces her to consult a doctor, who offers advice and suggests a stringent diet. In most cases of obesity it is difficult for an obese person to adhere to a stringent diet, which contains less than 4.9 MJ (1200 kcals) per day, because previously she has eaten at least twice and often four times this amount of energy each day. In this she resembles a 'binge-eater'. She wants to keep to the diet but she is tempted to eat. The decision to keep to a diet becomes even harder when a severely obese person has already lost substantial weight. Every day, in every social situation, she has to make a decision, and keep to it, that she will not eat food which other people are eating freely. She knows that she should keep her weight down, for whatever reason she first chose to reduce her weight, but she finds it frustrating to do so. She begins to think about food, and to plan a diet. The more she plans, the more she becomes preoccupied with food and the harder it is for her to keep to her diet. She may decide to abandon all attempts to diet, or may start binge-eating. Another choice is to seek to have some form of operation which will protect her at least partially from eating readily available food.

Eating disorders

The main key to weight loss is the motivation to keep permanently to a strict diet. It is also evident that most obese people must have eaten more food over the years than non-obese people or they would not be so fat.

In these two respects, obesity is an eating disorder, and its correction must involve methods by which the obese person finds it 'better', psychologically and physically, to reduce weight than to remain obese. The treatment of obesity therefore involves the person in changing her eating habits.

Further evidence that obesity is an eating disorder are the comments made by severely obese patients when placed on low-energy diets. Most have adverse emotional reactions. The main problems are a preoccupation with food (65-75 per cent), irritability (60-70 per cent), nervousness (40-50 per cent), and depression (35-45 per cent). These symptoms are similar to those voiced by bulimic patients and women who have anorexia nervosa.

Obesity can be defined in several ways, some of which require complex investigations and are only practical in research. Other definitions are less complicated, and enable a person to determine if she is obese. A simple and effective method is to use the Quetelet Index (W/H^2) (see p. 14). Using the index, four groups (or grades) can be identified:

Grade   0 : W/H^2 = 19-24.9   : Normal range of weight
Grade   I : W/H^2 = 25-29.9   : Overweight
Grade II : W/H^2 = 30-39.9   : Obesity
Grade III : W/H^2 = 40 or more : Severe, or morbid obesity

Generally overweight and obesity are defined as an excess of body fat, but a few very muscular men may be classified as overweight (on the W/H^2 formula) although they have no excess of body fat. However, the W/H^2 ratio of these men does not exceed 29, so they are not obese, by definition, although they may appear overweight. They can be differentiated from other overweight people relatively easily (Fig. 7, p. 15).

The grades are to some extent arbitrary, but help to emphasize that with increasing weight, distortions of the person's life-style may occur and help may be sought. When the person's weight places her in the classification of morbid obesity, medical conditions which are potentially life-threatening become more common and help is more urgently required.

As mentioned earlier (p. 14) the formula W/H^2 can also be used to define underweight and emaciation:

Grade — 1 : 15-18.9 : underweight
Grade — 2 : less than 15 : emaciation.

Those women in Grade — 2, who have no physical illness are generally suffering from anorexia nervosa.

3

Why do eating disorders occur?

What made me anorexic in the first instance seems to be unimportant to what keeps me as thin as I am. I've come to the right conclusion that my anorexia is just a bad habit and a crutch for any failings I may wish to excuse myself from making.

In spite of a considerable amount of research in the past three decades no consensus has been obtained to answer the question: Why do some adolescents have an eating disorder? Three explanations have been advanced, but none of them has been proved conclusively. They are (1) the combined biological and learning theory explanation, (2) the psychological explanation, and (3) the social explanation.

THE COMBINED BIOLOGICAL AND LEARNING THEORY EXPLANATION

From the earliest days of its life the quality of care a mother gives to her baby, and the love she lavishes on the baby are related at least indirectly to the amount of fat covering its body. A chubby baby is seen by the mother and her neighbours as a well-cared-for baby. In childhood, too, the provision of substantial amounts of food, often rich in refined carbohydrates and fat, is seen as a way of showing love for children, as well as ensuring that they are adequately nourished. In our culture, which has an abundance of food, children learn to increase progressively the amount of food they eat, and often increase the quantity of energy they ingest beyond that needed for growth, body functions, and the demands of exercise. In the three years before puberty, a biological spurt of growth occurs, and the food intake is increased still further.

Studies have shown that in boys the energy requirements for growth, and the spurt in growth, occur at about the age of 15; and because boys increase their muscle mass after this age, additional energy continues to

23

be needed. The growth spurt in girls occurs between the ages of 12 and 14, earlier than that of boys, and the girl's energy requirements peak over the same period. By the age of 16, the girl's energy requirements have fallen considerably, as females do not increase their muscle mass like boys. If the girl continues to eat the quantity of food she ate in early adolescence, obesity is inevitable. As she becomes increasingly aware of her body weight, she learns that she can control weight gain either by dieting or by using other measures which will help her to stop her absorbing the food she eats. On the other hand, some adolescents may reject the need to control their weight and may enjoy eating, while limiting the amount of energy expended in exercise. Inevitably this will lead to obesity. Some of the adolescents who diet and control their weight successfully may become so concerned about food and about weight control that their eating behaviour escapes from what is considered 'normal', and they decide to pursue thinness – becoming anorexia nervosa victims. Some of those who diet unsuccessfully either develop bulimia or become obese.

Case history: Vera

Vera first became concerned about her weight when she was aged 14 and started dieting. However her preoccupation with food caused her to gain weight in spite of the diet she had chosen. She was teased about her body by her friends and in an attempt to lose weight effectively began taking large quantities of laxatives when she was 16. Soon after she began to abuse laxatives, her menstrual periods ceased. The next year, a series of family problems and her continued concern about her body image induced her to adhere to a weight-reducing diet (1200 kcals a day) with resultant weight loss. By the age of 18 her weight had stabilized at the level she desired and has been maintained, with fluctuations of 2–6 lb (1–3 kg), for the past five years

Case history: Kate

Kate began to 'watch her weight' when she was at boarding school, as did many of her contemporaries. However, the nature of the food and the discipline imposed on the students limited her ability to control her weight. She left school at 18, having passed the Higher School Certificate, and became increasingly conscious of her weight. She decided that she wanted to lose weight by 'avoiding eating rubbish'. She was now at university, and began binge-eating, interspersing the bulimia with stringent dieting, which resulted in wide swings of weight

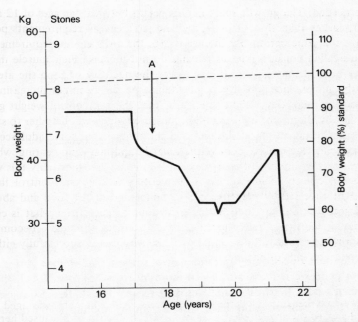

Fig. 8. Robin started dieting at the age of 14. By the age of 17 she had developed anorexia nervosa (A) and this has persisted in spite of treatment since that date.

In an attempt to control her weight gain, at the age of 19 she began to self-induce vomiting and abused both laxatives and diuretics. This behaviour coincided with a decision to leave university and to move to another city to take up fashion modelling. To some extent her behaviour controlled the swings in her weight, but she continued to have episodes of binge-eating, although these became less frequent, but it was not until she was aged 24 that she achieved a body weight in the low range of 'normal'. She has since stabilized at this weight by dieting, and no longer uses potentially dangerous methods of losing weight.

Onset of severe weight loss can also follow a period of sensible dieting with realistic weight loss or, in some of the younger patients, it appears to occur immediately, with no prior unsuccessful or realistic attempts. On the other hand, the young woman may reject the need to be or to become thin and may continue eating the quantity of food she has learned to eat and enjoys eating. If she was fat during early adolescence, the degree of obesity will increase. Obesity occurs in some families, and may be due to the family having a continuing fantasy that 'our family have always had healthy appetites and have been large people'. A child brought up in such a family is comfortable overeating and becoming obese because she can share an identity with the other members of her family. She has no need to limit her food intake in adolescence to conform with prevailing fashions because the strong influence of her family outweighs those of prevailing fashion.

THE PSYCHOLOGICAL EXPLANATION

Because eating is such a basic instinct it has been postulated that those people who suffer from an eating disorder have an identifiable personality, being more obsessional or neurotic than normal eaters. Some studies, using personality questionnaires, suggest that women suffering from anorexia nervosa are indeed more 'neurotic' or 'obessional' than women whose weight is in the 'desirable range'. The studies also suggest that those women who have lost weight by dieting and excessive exercise are more introverted, more anxious, and more dependent than women whose weight is normal or women with anorexia nervosa who use self-induced vomiting and purgation as methods of losing weight. No distinctive personality profiles are available for obese women.

The main problems about accepting the psychological explanation are: first, that many women who have anorexia nervosa or bulimia are found after careful testing to have 'normal' personalities and secondly, the personality scores of normal people and those who suffer from eating disorders overlap considerably. This may mean that the tests are too crude to identify a personality problem; or that the psychological explanation has no foundation.

An extension of this theory of a personality defect is the suggestion that some obese women use eating as a substitute for love. A person who feels lonely, empty, and unloved unless she has constant company, may eat to compensate. The emptiness of her life is soothed if she takes food to fill her empty stomach. The more she eats the more complete and full (or fulfilled) she feels. Food, and particularly beverages

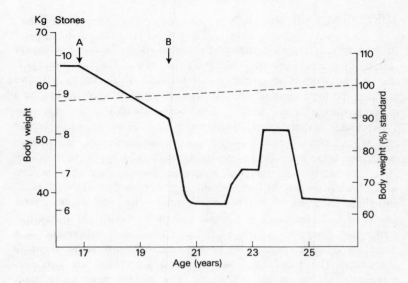

Fig. 9. Cheryl felt herself to be overweight when she was aged 17 and started dieting. At that time her weight was 110 per cent of the standard weight (A). The dieting resulted in a slow weight loss until the age of 20, when she broke up with her boy friend and had a sudden weight loss, leading to a diagnosis of anorexia nervosa (B).

such as milk or beer, become mainstays of her life, suppressing lack of self-esteem, and providing satisfaction. As she becomes increasingly obese she develops a need to remain obese, and avoid the resurgence of her feeling of inadequacy.

Furthermore, according to the personality defect theory, some women suffering from anorexia nervosa have a fear of 'growing up' and of becoming physically and sexually mature. By avoiding eating, the woman's body contours become those of a pre-pubertal child, her menstrual periods either do not start or cease, she is able to withdraw from the social occasions which make her ill at ease and anxious, and is able to deny her sexuality. This explanation may apply to a few anorexia nervosa patients, but in most cases of eating disorders the concept does not apply.

27

THE SOCIAL EXPLANATION

In Western culture two contrasting messages about food and eating are offered by society, and particularly by the media. The first message is that a slim woman is successful, attractive, healthy, happy, fit, and popular. To become slim, with all that this implies, is deemed to be a major pursuit of many women. The second message is that eating is a pleasurable activity which meets many needs in addition to relieving hunger, and women have a right to have these needs met. In women's magazines these two contrasting messages tend to appear inextricably mixed. In nearly every issue the magazines publish 'exciting' new diets which 'guarantee weight loss with minimum discomfort or motivation', and these diets are often followed by recipes for, and superb photographs of, luscious cakes and foods with rich sauces. It is difficult to watch television without being confronted by an advertisement for a substitute diet-food alternating with a fast food advertisement, or its equivalent. The social (and usually family) pressures are also contradictory: you must eat everything other people give you but you must not get fat.

The provision of food is seen in our culture as a major sign of caring; and sharing food at a meal is seen as one of the prime social contacts. These cultural imperatives place a burden on a mother to provide abundant quantities of food, and on her loving daughter or son to eat that food. It is not surprising that in the face of the psychological bombardment of two contradictory messages, most young women diet. Some become 'foodaholics' and develop bulimia. Others become preoccupied with food and the avoidance of weight gain, developing bulimia or anorexia nervosa. Some decide that dieting is too disturbing to their way of life and return to eating more food than they require, becoming obese. These women may also find obesity protective against acceding to current social attitudes to sexuality, which they fear. Hidden in a fat body, they give the message that they are not attractive and do not want to form a sexual relationship.

4

Eating disorders and sexuality

Often I used to go out and eat for my sensual sexual experience of the day. I actually would be turned on by it.

The sexual knowledge, attitudes and behaviour of women with eating disorders covers a broad spectrum. This is not surprising as many are over-concerned about their body image and their relationships with others. We have found that there is an association between eating behaviour and sexual behaviour of the women we have studied. We have identified four categories: sexuality denied; unsure of sexuality; sexually passive; and sexually active.

SEXUALITY DENIED

The woman avoids challenge to her sexuality and suppresses her sexual feelings. She has negative attitudes to puberty, menstruation, masturbation, and sexual intercourse. These attitudes may be aggravated by her lack of knowledge of her genital anatomy, of menstruation, of contraception, and of sexual behaviour. She avoids reading about sexuality and is rigid and obsessional in her attitudes to life. She avoids looking at her body in a mirror, and does not touch her genitals. She uses external sanitary pads for menstrual protection and has never attempted to use tampons. Most of the women in this group have no sexual experience, and neither masturbate nor date. They become embarrassed if a discussion relates to sex, but often wish that they had a close companion. These women lose weight exclusively by strict dieting and exercise, and often are emaciated.

Case history: Clarissa

Clarissa is aged 28, is an only child, and is a highly intelligent, personable, neatly dressed woman, but rather obsessional and anxious. She finds it difficult to relate socially. She learned about menstruation when she was 13 from her mother, who was embarrassed and not very informative. Six months later she had her first menstrual period. She was ashamed and embarrassed about menstruating, and described her periods as 'messy', 'dirty', 'disgusting', and 'inconvenient'. She was unable to touch herself 'down there', and used sanitary pads, which she continues to use. She feels unable to use tampons. She received no information about sexuality or sexual intercourse from her mother, and felt unable to ask anyone else because of her shyness. She has avoided reading any books about sexuality, and says that 'there is no point because I wouldn't remember any of the information'.

At the age of 20 she had her first relationship, but it broke up after two years of courting because she believed that the man was 'making demands on her', and because she couldn't cope with his desire for heavy petting. She has since avoided any physical contact with a man. She finds it difficult to say words describing sexual functions, and found kissing 'disgusting' although she permitted her boyfriend to kiss her occasionally. The idea of sexual intercourse revolts her, particularly as she would be forced to look at and touch the man's genitals. She has a dread of exposing her body and of looking at her breasts, abdomen, or thighs in a mirror.

She began dieting soon after the relationship ended. Her object in dieting was to reduce the size of her breasts (which she saw as large and ugly although her boyfriend had complimented her on their shape) and to take weight off her abdomen. By the age of 23 she was considerably underweight and her menstrual periods had ceased. She says that she is pleased about this as she hated menstruating and she uses her thinness to avoid social situations and sexual challenges. She is 'uptight' and fastidious in her appearance and at work, her employer referring to her as 'a most excellent secretary'.

In the past five years she has had episodes of dramatic weight loss, due to stringent dieting alone, which have required admissions to hospital for refeeding. She has never induced vomiting, having a fear of its effects, nor does she abuse laxatives or diuretics. Her rigid dieting and her sexual attitudes appear to be part of a constant preoccupation with 'self control' and a desire for perfection. She is not sure what masturbation is and would never attempt it. She denies any sexual feelings and says she has never accepted that she 'could have a libido'. However, the thought that she might be a lesbian causes her to avoid female company. She is 'disgusted' by homosexuality. She is often lonely and wishes for a male or female companion, but avoids making friends, believing herself unable to cope with an intimacy that could lead to a sexual challenge. Amenorrhoea has been 'a relief' which she hopes will continue.

UNSURE OF SEXUALITY

These women appear to use their eating behaviour to delay sexual encounters until they feel that they are ready for them. The woman tends to find it difficult to form a warm, mature relationship, although she may marry, when she tends to be dependent on her husband. She is anxious to conform and has conflicts about her sexual feelings and her sexual behaviour, always trying to be what she believes is 'normal'. She is shy. She may masturbate occasionally but worries because it may not be 'right' to masturbate. If she is given reassurance that her sexual behaviour is 'normal' she begins to enjoy it. She is shy, and although she may look at her naked body in a mirror, does not feel comfortable when doing it. She is also shy about menstrual protection and prefers sanitary pads to tampons, as she finds the latter 'difficult' to insert. Her anxiety about vaginal insertion extends to sexual intercourse, which usually first takes place at an older age than average. She believes that she is not easily aroused, but sometimes reaches orgasm either by clitoral stimulation or during sexual intercourse. She would like to learn about sexuality but is too shy to initiate a discussion.

Women in this group lose weight predominantly by dieting and exercising. If they decide to use laxatives or diuretics, they only take small quantities for short periods of time. Usually they have anorexia nervosa but may be obese.

Case history: Samantha

Samantha is aged 26 and is an attractive 'elfin' woman who is dependent on others and needs continual reassurance and approval about her relationship with both sexes. She learnt about menstruation and sexuality from a book (given to her by her mother) when she was 12 years old. She went to a boarding school run by nuns, and was worried when her menstrual periods failed to start, as all the other girls in her class were menstruating. She became increasingly anxious and apprehensive about starting to menstruate, and was embarrassed when, at the age of 15, her first menstrual period began during a dancing class. Sex education was not provided at school, but she was told that it was wrong and unhealthy to masturbate. When she tried masturbation she felt guilty and ashamed and did not repeat the experience. During her last two years at school, she dieted, unsuccessfully, with school friends, and her weight increased slightly, although it stayed within the 'desirable' range. She was self-conscious about the small size of her breasts,

31

and the fact that whilst her school friends *needed* bras she just *wore* one.

She left school and entered university, where she began dieting. This resulted in weight loss and her menstrual periods ceased, which pleased her, saying she 'felt lucky they had stopped because she hated them'. Towards the end of the first year in university, she formed a relationship with another student. She knew herself to be sexually ignorant and although her ignorance worried her she did not seek any sexual information. She permitted nothing more than kissing in the relationship. The relationship lasted two months, and after it ended she continued to diet strictly and lose weight. When she was 20 she met her future husband. By this time she was very thin. During their four year courtship she limited sexual contact to kissing, and occasional breast fondling, although she did not enjoy this because of the small size of her breasts and her guilt. Before the marriage at the age of 24, she visited her family doctor who induced 'menstruation' for two cycles, using hormones. She tried to use a tampon during the first episode of bleeding but reverted to pads as 'it was difficult and uncomfortable to put the thing in'. At marriage she was emaciated and fulfilled the criteria for anorexia nervosa. She had a romantic opinion about marriage and believed that once married she would 'blossom'. The first attempt at sexual intercourse was a 'dismal failure', which disillusioned her. Subsequent intercourse has often been painful and the couple tend to avoid sex. She alternates between blaming herself and her husband who she says is 'undersexed'. She has never discussed sex with him because of embarrassment and the belief that she is 'frigid'. When they have sexual intercourse, she tells him she enjoys it, and has fantasies of responding more if they could vary positions during sexual intercourse, but feels too inhibited to suggest the idea. She has never had an orgasm during sexual intercourse, but says she can sometimes reach orgasm if her husband stimulates her clitoris, although she believes it is 'not right to do it'. Her husband enjoys swimming but she refuses to go with him as she thinks she is too thin and is embarrassed about her small breasts. At times she wishes she was 'soft and cuddly' like most women.

SEXUALLY PASSIVE

Women in this group (which include those who have anorexia nervosa, bulimia, or who are obese) also appear to use their eating disorder to avoid having to make a sexual commitment until they want to. The woman's eating behaviour offers her a chance to place an 'intermittent moratorium' on her sexual activity. She experiences wide swings in weight, binge-eating alternating with periods of fasting or strict dieting. If she is bulimic, she rarely reaches a low weight and if she does she maintains the low weight only for a short period of time, before binge-eating and gaining weight. Between underweight and overweight episodes, women in this group become involved in sexual relationships, but are unresponsive, denying that they enjoy their experiences. Because they do not wish for a commitment they tend to choose partners who are married, and with whom a long-term relationship is not possible. In the relationship they prefer to cuddle and be held, and accept sexual intercourse to achieve this rather than because they enjoy the experience. They are able to touch their genitals and use tampons for menstrual protection, but their ability to look at their body depends on their weight at the time.

Case history: Harriet

Harriet who is aged 25 is an attractive obese young woman who desperately wanted to lose weight in order to attract a boyfriend and to 'live a normal life'. Before she had menstruated (when she was 13 years old) her mother had told her to expect 'a brown spot on her pants' and had taken her to a 'mother and daughter night'. For two years she suffered from pain and vomiting with her menstrual periods and wished to be rid of them. She used external pads until changing to tampons when she was 18. At the age of 14 she had a brief lesbian relationship at school but felt it 'did nothing' for her. When she was 16, she decided to 'stop eating rubbish' and reduced her weight by dieting. At the age of 17 she applied for and was accepted for a teachers training course and began alternating between binge-eating and stringent dieting. In addition she abused laxatives. During the course and subsequently when teaching in primary school the eating behaviour caused at least five rapid swings in weight. She wanted to lose weight from her 'bottom, stomach, and thighs' and would look at her body in a mirror when her weight was low, but avoided looking when she was 'fat'. She dressed to camouflage her body when she was obese but not when she was thin. Over a three-month period her weight could vary from 7 stone (44 kg) to 9 stone (57 kg).

Throughout the six years her menstrual pattern was quite irregular and she did not bother to record when she menstruated. She considered premarital sex 'normal' and wished to lose her virginity 'as quickly as possible', in order to 'satisfy curiosity', 'to rebel against' her parents and to achieve 'maturity'. She believed sexual intercourse was necessary to attract and keep a boyfriend. At the age of 19 she had intercourse six weeks after meeting her first boyfriend. She described her first ex-perience of penetration as 'fantastic because of the pain'. Later experiences were not painful but 'never satisfying'. During the 12 months of her first sexual relationship her weight fluctuated within the normal range. She used the contraceptive pill throughout the relationship. She ended the relationship because of recurrence of bulimia and consequent weight increase. Renewed dieting lowered her weight but when she began binge-eating her weight continued to rise. Her second sexual contact was during a five-month stabilization of weight. She had hoped to gain a friend by agreeing to have sexual intercourse but felt obliged to terminate the relationship after renewed binge-eating. Desperation with weight gain culminated in a suicide attempt by an overdose of sleeping tablets. She has 'never really enjoyed' oro-genital sex and prefers to be the recipient. She will only use a passive, supine position for sexual intercourse. She feels guilty about masturbating and states that she has turned to binge-eating as a 'substitute'. After the commencement of treatment and an initial weight reduction she maintained her weight within the normal range for 10 months during which time she resumed sexual activity with two older, married men which she enjoyed but found sexually unrewarding. She ceased to abuse laxatives and the frequency of bulimia was reduced from weekly to monthly episodes. These relationships were termi-nated during a brief episode of bulimic behaviour with a resultant rise in weight of 8 lb (4 kg). Her weight has subsequently been stable within the normal range for six months and sexual activity has resumed.

SEXUALLY ASSERTIVE

Women in this group mirror their eating behaviour, which consists of binge-eating followed by episodes of self-induced vomiting and laxative abuse, with their sexual behaviour. They are unable to form a long-term relationship and have frequent casual sexual encounters. They usually have had their first sexual experience at an early age; they masturbate and have oral sex, but are rather negative about both of these. They talk about sex freely and have no anxiety about being naked, either when alone or with others. They tend to be histrionic, and socially active, but underlying this is a feeling of loneliness.

Case history: Brenda

Brenda is an attractive well-groomed blonde of 24 who has a rather histrionic manner. She is preoccupied with sex and likes talking and reading about it. However, she is preoccupied by doubts about her sexuality. She says she only feels feminine when her stomach is completely empty. Her mother discussed sex and masturbation with her before she went to boarding school at 12 years of age. She and a girlfriend would often explore and embrace each other in bed. She started menstruating when she was aged 14, which she described as 'unpleasant and a nuisance'; and it was associated with cramps requiring bed rest. She has continued to feel that her menstrual periods are 'hateful' and wishes she could 'do away with them'. For the first two menstrual cycles she used external pads and has since used tampons exclusively. She felt 'pressurized' into first intercourse at age 15 and found penetration painful and unpleasant. Subsequently she has enjoyed intercourse at times, including 'rough' intercourse. She sometimes reaches orgasm. She regrets having had sex outside marriage and wishes she could have been a 'virgin bride'. She has had many casual sexual partners since the age of 15. Following a 'pregnancy scare' at age 17, she developed an increased fear of pregnancy, dreading changes in body shape and the pain of childbirth, but did not use contraceptives. At age 18 she became more conscious of her weight, and dieting by avoiding 'rubbish foods'. She became engaged when she was 19, but decided she didn't really like her fiancé, and broke off the relationship. When the man married her closest girlfriend she was deeply upset and decided to move to another city where she could 'start again'. Her progress there was a disaster at first. She began binge-eating and because her weight increased she began to self-induce vomiting, and abused laxatives. She found it impossible to keep to a diet and began to drink alcohol to excess. She was very social, hated being alone and said that on her 'good days she was the life of the party'. Increased vomiting and purging led to a steady decrease in her weight. At the lower weight she became intensely preoccupied, almost narcissistic, about her appearance and the size of her abdomen, her hips, and her thighs. Because of her appearance she obtained a job as a cosmetic representative which she enjoyed. She had multiple sexual relationships and began taking the pill. When taking oral contraceptives her menstrual periods became scanty, which pleased her. By the age of 24 her preoccupation with her body and her weight increased and she started dieting strictly, induced vomiting and abused laxatives with the result that her body weight fell and she became emaciated. Her menstrual periods ceased when her weight was low, but she continued with multiple sexual relationships, which often involved oral and anal sex, although the latter revolted her. She says that she 'craves orgasm' and tries to get it any way she can, masturbating in the absence of other outlets. She has now been binge-eating and vomiting for five years. She has frequent invitations to parties and frequents bars and restaurants. She avoids eating before going out and prefers to wear loose fitting clothes. After returning home she induces vomiting. She feels she is most likely to vomit in a situation where she fears both sexual challenge and a temptation to 'overeat'.

5

Investigation of eating disorders

I don't want to be like this, but what I eat still rules my life so that at times every working minute seems occupied with thoughts of food and the day passes in the measured times between when I last ate and when I'll eat again. I'm still plagued with guilt about everything I consume unless I nearly fast. I dream of the perfect day when I have no appetite, no thought, desire, or temptation for food or to eat. I often despair of ever finding a solution.

Weight loss and excessive weight gain may be caused by several physical and psychiatric conditions. These have to be excluded before the diagnosis of an eating disorder is made. For example, starvation causes emaciation, as does advanced terminal cancer and tuberculosis; gross obesity may be due to a brain tumour or to an endocrine disorder. These conditions, and others, are excluded by obtaining a good history of the disorder and by an appropriate physical examination by a doctor. This examination includes the careful measurement of the person's height and weight, and this is related to Average Body Weight tables (see Appendix, p. 154) or the calculation of weight divided by the square of the height is made (Quetelet Index) (p. 15).

Most people with eating disorders either have a fear of becoming fat, or are obese and perceive themselves as ugly, massive, undesirable, or flabby. Both groups have poor self-esteem and a poor body image. For this reason it is important for the doctor to make a psychological evaluation of the patient before starting any treatment. There are many scales which help in this, each having its adherents. Many are complex and contradictory, but a few simple questions provide much useful information.

The purpose of the questions is to try to establish whether the patient is prepared to alter her eating behaviour, to lose or gain weight, and if she has sufficiently high motivation and fortitude to make the changes. If her motivation is low, a great deal of time will be expended, both by the doctor and the patient, with little benefit.

The following questions have been tested and found to be helpful in establishing a patient's motivation to change her disordered eating behaviour.

1. *Do you really want to change your eating behaviour?*

If the patient is unwilling to change her eating behaviour there is no point in starting treatment. In mild cases her enjoyment of her present behaviour may outweigh the long-term consequences of emaciation or obesity. This implies that in some cases the person has to get worse, becoming even more emaciated, or more obese, before she is sufficiently motivated to accept treatment. In extreme cases when the illness may threaten her life pressure must be placed on her to accept treatment.

2. *What is your occupation?*

Certain jobs which involve business entertaining, catering, extensive travelling, shift work, or long periods of relative inactivity and boredom make dieting difficult. Knowledge of the patient's occupation helps the physician to suggest strategies for resisting the compulsion to eat. Occupations which require the patient to be thin, such as fashion modelling or ballet dancing have to be accepted, and treatment may have to be modified so that the desired weight fits in with the occupation. Another example is the woman whose occupation is involved with food preparation or who is a waitress, because her occupation may reinforce her preoccupation with food.

3. *What is your weight now?*

Assessment of the patient's current weight and her 'desirable weight' enables the physician to estimate how long it will take for the woman to achieve her desirable weight if her motivation is high and if she adheres to the recommended diet, whether this is to achieve refeeding or weight reduction. Knowledge of the woman's present weight may also give some indication about further medical investigations which should be made to avoid aggravating a possible vitamin deficiency or a metabolic disturbance, such as low blood potassium, which could cause cardiac arrest.

4. *What weight would you like to achieve?*

Investigation of eating disorders

It is important for this to be discussed as the patient may have unrealistic expectations, which may require to be modified. It is also helpful to explore the reason a particular weight was selected as the 'desirable' personal weight.

5. *What is the heaviest you have ever been?*
This question establishes if the person has previously attempted to reduce, or to increase her weight; whether she failed or achieved partial success; and how she coped.

6. *What is the lowest weight you reached?*
The question has greater applicability to people who have anorexia nervosa and gives an indication of weight changes, at least those reported by the patient.

7. *Have you maintained your weight over a period of at least six months without much effort?*
This question gives a reasonable indication of a weight which the patient could aim for, and it may help her recognize that she can maintain a body weight without being preoccupied with food.

8. *How do you think changing your weight will change your life-style?*
Many patients try to generalize in answer to this question saying that 'I'll probably feel better' or 'I read that I should lose weight'. The question requires to be answered more specifically, and the patient should try to state clearly what things she hopes to do after weight change which cannot be done while she is emaciated or obese. It may help the patient if she makes a list of the reasons why she wants to gain or to lose weight. She may find difficulty in answering this question at the beginning of treatment, but later, with more insight into her eating disorder, this may help her to understand her eating problem. As an example, a patient who has anorexia nervosa who changes her weight may feel that she will lose control, not only of her eating behaviour but of her life-style, and may also lose the feeling of 'safety' she had when her body weight was low.

9. *Are you on a diet at present?*
If the answer is yes, it is important to establish exactly what the diet contains, and how rigorous the patient has been in keeping to it.

For example, many obese people try new fashionable 'fad' diets, but the diet is not really effective and the dieter has insufficient motivation to keep to it. Information about the patient's chosen diet is even more valuable when she has anorexia nervosa or bulimia. Starvation diets are more likely to end in an episode of binge-eating than 'sensible' diets, rather in the way a person who misses breakfast and lunch because of work or other circumstances, feels hungry when dinner-time approaches and is likely to eat more at dinner than normal. It is also useful to find what the diet contains, as some 'health' foods contain considerable amounts of sugar, and many obese people do not consider beverages as food, although they contain sugar. Even 'low-calorie' foods and drinks provide a considerable amount of energy if the person eats or drinks quantities of them, believing that they will not put on weight.

Many women with eating disorders lose their perception of how much they need to eat, or not to eat, if they wish to maintain a constant weight. Obese people tend to overestimate their food needs, while patients with anorexia nervosa tend to underestimate how much they should eat to maintain a constant weight. Bulimia patients usually underestimate their requirements because they do not include the food eaten during a binge as normal eating.

10. *Have you previously tried dieting to lose or to gain weight?*

If the person has dieted previously and has failed to gain or to lose weight while dieting or has kept to the diet for only a short time, it is important to establish this fact, as well as finding why previous attempts at dieting were abandoned.

11. *Have you used any other ways apart from dieting to lose weight?*

People who have failed to lose weight because they have not kept to their diet often try other methods such as self-induced vomiting, or laxative or diuretic abuse, or excessive exercise in an attempt to lose weight. This applies to bulimia patients, anorexia nervosa patients, and to obese patients. In fact over 40 weight-losing behaviours were reported in a recent study made in Sydney (Table 3, p. 17). Some of the methods are potentially dangerous, but most patients only resort to them when simpler methods have apparently failed. It may help the patient understand her eating disorder if the reason why the methods failed to work is talked about or thought about. As some of the methods are socially unacceptable it may be difficult for some patients to admit that they have used them. But the patient and her therapist should try to explore them, since much of the management of eating disorders is directed to changing eating and weight-losing behaviours. The question also enables the physician to decide if further medical and laboratory investigations are needed.

12. *If you keep strictly to a diet, how quickly do you think you should lose weight?*

Unrealistic expectations (usually obtained from reading about 'fad' or crash diets) can be clarified by asking this question. For example, many people know that on a strict diet it is relatively easy to lose 7 lb (3 kg) in the first week, but expect to be able to continue losing weight at this rate which is unrealistic (this is discussed further on p. 122). They find that they do not lose weight rapidly after the first week and may give up the diet assuming that it is 'no good'. It also helps the patient to know that the weekly weight loss or weight gain may fluctuate even though she has adhered to the diet. A person who says 'I have only to look at food to put on weight' is playing games with herself, and is either eating snacks, practising 'picking behaviour'; so is a person who says to herself that 'a piece of cake, or a chocolate, won't do any harm' — and goes on eating pieces of cake and chocolates.

13. *Do you expect to lose weight without dieting?*

The question may seem stupid at first. Of course, the person will answer that she does not: but when the subject is explored further it will be found that most people seek magic cures for obesity or for losing weight while continuing to binge-eat. Many of these women spend considerable quantities of money following 'fad' diets or attending various courses guaranteeing painless weight reduction.

14. *Are you taking any medication at present?*

This question is designed to determine what medication the patient has been given, why the medications were prescribed or bought, and whether they are really needed. It explores the matters raised in Question 11.

15. *Tell me about your family?*

The question is deliberately vague. It seeks to determine if the

41

parents of the patient were fat; whether siblings or children are fat; what sort of life the family leads; what pressures are put on the person by the other family members; who does the cooking and who the shopping; if other family members are dieting. Family dynamics may have a considerable influence on the patient's opinion of herself and disclosure may help in changing eating behaviour.

16. *Tell me about your life-style*

The information obtained from this question enables the therapist to decide on the strategy which is most likely to succeed in inducing the person to change her eating behaviour and to persist with the new eating habit.

6

Management of eating disorders

When this all started, I used to always use a knife to eat an apple, and a teaspoon to eat cereal or desert – I suppose it took longer, and therefore felt as if I was eating more. I always left a bit of potato/rice/ noodles on my plate, no matter how much was served to me – as a test of willpower. The whole exercise of putting on weight, to me, is a breakdown of my iron willpower, because I know only too well that I enjoy eating. That is what still revolts me – the amount of food actually to be consumed in order to put on one stone. I've always maintained that I would so much prefer to have one stone in weight 'sewn' on instead of having to 'eat' it on.

Eating disorders occur because a person loves food and either seeks to control this love rigorously (anorexia nervosa) or intermittently (bulimia), or has little or no control over eating (obesity). It follows from this observation that the reversion of an eating disorder to 'normal' eating depends on several decisions. The first is that the person perceives that she has an eating disorder. The second is that the person believes that if the disordered eating continues it may cause a serious problem to her life-style or to her health, or both. In other words, she has to decide that the benefit, or reward, of changing the disordered eating behaviour exceeds that of the cost of continuing with it, at a physical, psycho-logical, and social level. Having made these decisions, she has to ex-perience or show a readiness to change her present eating habits. This implies that she will accept the help given, but understands that the change will only occur if she is prepared to achieve the change herself. It is relatively easy to lose (or to gain) weight so that it lies within the desirable range: it is much harder to *maintain* the weight within the desirable range.

To achieve weight alteration and to stabilize it within the desirable range, the person has to change her life-style and eating behaviour and habits. It is important to be aware that eating disorders do not exist in isolation, they are a result of altered eating behaviour, which in turn may be a reaction to events in a person's life. Because of this, treatment must take care of the other problems and needs of the individual, and help the person to learn to cope with the problems in ways other than resorting to eating or avoiding eating. The aim of treatment is to help obese people to avoid eating excessively, to help anorexia nervosa patients to enjoy eating and to reduce their fear of becoming fat, and to help bulimia patients alter their eating behaviour. If the individual is to achieve the needed change she requires motivation, fortitude, persistence, and a continuing stimulus to change. This will only be achieved when she becomes aware of the factors – physiological, psychological, social, and familial – which induce her to continue her disordered eating. She also needs to become aware that what triggered the disordered eating habit is not necessarily the reason why it is continuing. For example, if a disturbed family relationship was one of the factors which led to the onset of anorexia nervosa, it may be necessary not only to explore this relationship but also to use other treatments. She may have to learn that although she has a morbid fear of becoming fat, it is safe for her to try to increase her weight, and that she will not lose control of her eating and other behaviour. On the other hand, unless a grossly obese individual can be induced to lose her urge to eat, starting a strict diet may lead her to take one of two actions. First, she may pander to her urge to eat and so break her diet. At first the food gives her pleasure, but then guilt may follow and lead to depression. Alternatively, she may keep to her diet and suffer 'stress' because she does not accede to her urge to eat. This can lead to anger, frustration, or depression. If an obese person continues eating because of loneliness, boredom, or stress at work this must be examined.

The obese person must be provided with a comprehensive dietary plan which is easy to understand and to follow, and must clearly understand why she has to take in less energy than she expends. The diet must be presented in a positive way. This means that the patient learns (or is taught) to choose appropriate foods rather than being instructed to avoid inappropriate foods; and the chosen diet must not distort her eating patterns too greatly. The place of exercise as a method of weight loss must be understood, and the effects of taking laxatives, diuretics, and self-induced vomiting must be comprehended clearly by the patient.

Management of eating disorders

As far as is possible the patient and her therapist have to agree to try and be honest with each other. The problem is that patients with eating disorders tend to 'play games' and to manipulate the therapist. In spite of this the patient should try to answer honestly that she is complying with the diet they have jointly chosen and should try to discuss how her altered eating behaviour is affecting other behaviour. As it is important to 'track' changes in behaviour as well as of weight during treatment the patient must be able to have confidence in and trust the therapist.

Changes in weight can be tracked by weighing and, in obese patients, by measuring the skinfold thickness changes or by using a Weight Reduction Index* which is as follows:

$$\frac{\text{Weight loss (in kg)}}{\text{Weight in excess of desirable weight}} \times 100$$

The behavioural changes can be found by careful questioning by the therapist and their implications discussed.

The therapist will discuss the place of 'self-help' groups as many patients benefit from them although others are uncomfortable in such groups. Self-help groups, such as Weight Watchers International, TOPS (Taking Off Pounds Sensibly), and Overeaters Anonymous are used mainly to help obese people lose weight, but could be helpful for people trying to gain weight. They have several advantages. (1) the leaders of the group have been able to alter their own eating habits and have achieved and maintained their weight goal: they are therefore able to serve as a model for the other members of the group; (2) the person finds it easy to join and to leave the group: which may be more difficult if she is treated by a therapist, as she may feel an obligation to the therapist; (3) the group exerts a 'dynamic effect' which may help the person counter the psychological and social pressures which encourage relapse; (4) the method helps the person feel that she has achieved the change of eating behaviour by her own efforts without a

*The weight reduction quotient is more accurate. It is:

$$\text{Weight reduction quotient} = \frac{\text{Kg lost}}{\text{Kg overweight}} \times \frac{\text{Initial weight (kg)}}{\text{Desirable weight}} \times 100$$

45

'professional' taking over her treatment, although this negative effect is reduced if the professional is well-trained, skilled, and empathetic; (5) the person is not converted into a 'patient' with a 'disease'; and (6) usually the courses provided by self-help groups are cheaper than those provided by health professionals; a factor which may be of some importance for compliance.

The sufferer must continually be aware that changes in her life-style are as important as changes in weight, and that the two are inter-linked. She must also be aware that the decision to change her eating behaviour to achieve a 'desirable' weight has to be reinforced often throughout her life, and that she may need help and support at intervals to maintain her resolve and her weight, if she feels she may relapse. Success in reversing eating disorders cannot be claimed in short-term follow-up as many relapses occur. Follow-up has to be prolonged, usually for five to ten years.

THE ADVANTAGES OF HAVING AN EATING DISORDER

Women who have eating disorders may see advantages in continuing with 'abnormal' eating behaviour. The advantages may be perceived by the woman as being greater than the disadvantages of the disorder, so that she is more comfortable persisting with the behaviour than changing it. The advantages vary and depend on whether the person has anorexia nervosa, has bulimia, or is severely obese.

An eating disorder may become an all-absorbing hobby and lead to the exclusion of most other age-related activities. In this way the sufferer is able to avoid making decisions, and can reduce the challenges made on her. If the challenges are sexual, the woman may use her emaciation, or her obesity, to avoid them, claiming that her distorted body shape would repel rather than attract men. One of our patients said 'when my body weight is normal I am scared of people's expect-ations of me, and have to resist men who make advances. But when I am fat, I am able to avoid these problems'.

Other patients find that their emaciation, or obesity, makes other members of the family concerned. The woman becomes the centre of concern and induces the family to make expressions of love, and to go to great lengths to 'look after her'. In this way she may be able to manipulate the family and obtains satisfaction from her behaviour. Other women manipulate close relatives by adopting 'illness behaviour'. Because the woman is perceived by her relatives as being 'ill' she is looked after. She is able to feel dependent, without feeling guilty, and may use this 'illness' to avoid a social or a family situation. For example, one of our patients lost weight each year in November and December so that she could be admitted to hospital for Christmas rather than having to spend it with her family. Another patient used her illness to justify her behaviour towards her husband, saying that 'my husband knew that he was marrying a sick person. If I get better he may not like me and we may separate'. By being ill she forced her husband to concentrate on her needs to the exclusion of his needs.

In other cases the person uses her eating disorder to avoid discussion of other problems in her relationship with her husband or family, or to avoid going out to social functions, at which she is uncomfortable. The person's emaciation or obesity may be used as an excuse to avoid competition. One of our patients ceased competitive swimming at the age of 12 and began putting on weight. By the time she was 19 her weight had risen to 17 st (108 kg). She wrote:

All the girls were too competitive. I'm out of that now, and can get on with everyone. When I was swimming people picked on me if I didn't do as well as they expected me to have done. Now I can do what I like, and do the things I like well. Now I'm fat, I find that people come and talk to me. They can see I have a problem. They can see I have a weakness of character, or I wouldn't eat so much. They have problems too. Other people can't see their problems, but as my problem is obvious they feel comfortable with me.

Another of our patients wrote about her eating disorder:

I feel I have always needed the food to give me 'the rush' to make me high and happy. I know I use it as a protection barrier against experiencing and expressing emotional feeling with others and against physical and mental intimacy with a man. I have the need to break down this barrier and take charge of my life. You asked me what did I think would change if I lost the weight. I don't think the actual weight loss (or gain) would change anything, but if I could cease to look upon myself as a compulsive eater and feel relaxed about my food intake, then I feel I could tap the vitality and creativity that has eluded me all my life − I would feel I was functioning as a whole and not the several personalities I feel I am.

Obesity may also be a camouflage in families who are overweight. Being fat enables the person to fit in with the family and to behave as they do.

Some women feel a sense of achievement in being able to reduce their weight so that they become emaciated. One of our patients, aged 20, who had anorexia nervosa, and who had, in her words, 'done nothing with my life' wrote to us saying 'At least I've done one thing well. I enjoy being my Doctor's worst patient.'

Most people have an idealized view of how they should appear: they want to be socially attractive, happy and outgoing, and popular. When the person realizes that she cannot achieve her ideal, she may adopt disordered eating behaviour, either losing weight and becoming thin or gaining weight and becoming obese. In this way she has an excuse which explains why she can't achieve her ideal. But at these extremes of weight she looks in a mirror and doesn't like her body image. She then tries to return to the normal weight range, by dieting and other methods.

7

Anorexia nervosa

I just wish that anorexia would get the blazes out of my life! From 1977 to now, everything I do, have done or didn't do centres around my fear of food. For those of you not familiar with the demonic workings of anorexia – fear of food and getting fat are its basic elements.

Anorexia nervosa affects females fifteen times more commonly than males and usually begins during adolescence or in early adulthood. It is rare for the illness to occur for the first time to a woman who is over the age of 25, and if it does, the eating disorder is usually associated with severe mental or physical disease. Anorexia nervosa seems to be occurring more frequently among young women in the developed

Fig. 10. Anorexia nervosa

49

countries. Indeed, the illness affects one teenager in every 200, reaching a peak incidence of one in 100 among adolescents aged between 16 and 18.

Case history: Alison

Alison was a tall, slim girl, who at the age of 15 had begun dieting with the other members of her class at school. She did this to feel part of the group rather than because she needed to lose weight. She managed to stick to the diet better than most of her peers, her weight falling from 8 st 2 lb (52 kg) (90 per cent of Average Body Weight) to 7 st 2 lb (47 kg) (80 per cent of ABW). 'I was able to keep to the diet because my family are health freaks, and I began to feel guilty if I ate "bad fattening" foods.' About this time she began to be teased by the other girls about her small breasts and became self-conscious about them and her bottom, which she said 'stuck out too much'.

Alison was ambitious and wanted to do well at school. In her last two years she seldom went out to social events, because she felt she had to study, which she did conscientiously. 'Perhaps I was rather obsessional about study', she said, 'but I wanted to do well'. As well as studying hard, she cooked for the family, making cakes and biscuits (which she avoided eating) in addition to cooking the main meals. She perceived her household duties as helping her mother, who had a full time job, but her sister perceived them as trying to be a 'goody goody'.

She passed her school examinations and enrolled in a catering course because she enjoyed the practical aspects of cooking and preparing food. About this time she began to weigh herself each day, and continued to diet so that she became thinner. Her sister left home, and told Alison that in her opinion she had only 'lost weight to get all the attention of the family and put her sister's nose out of joint.' The sibling rivalry was marked.

Over the next two years, Alison continued with her course and proved an outstanding student. During this period her father's weight increased by about 2 st 2 lb (14 kg) whilst his daughter's weight continued to decline, so that at graduation Alison weighed 5 st (32 kg). Her father was diagnosed as having a high blood pressure and instructed to lose weight which he found difficult to do. Alison tried to help informing him what to eat, and worked out diets for him, 'counting the calories' of the food in the diets she devised.

She recognized that she was very thin and that she no longer menstruated, but felt she was eating as much as other people, and if she ate more she would 'put on weight rapidly and become fat'. She felt safe as long as her weight did not increase. She also felt it was wrong to eat more than others when 'there were so many starving people in the world'.

Anorexia nervosa

When she was 19 she visited a doctor about constipation which worried her and which she did not connect with her small intake of food. She was diagnosed as having anorexia nervosa and admitted to hospital for refeeding which was not successful. She responded to outpatient treatment and over seven months her weight increased to 6 st 13 lb (44 kg). She wanted to put on more weight but was worried that if she did she 'would lose control and become fat'. With persuasion and persistence she was induced to gain weight and by the age of 20 had stabilized at 7 st 10 lb (49 kg). She now believed that if her weight increased to 7 st 12 lb (50 kg) she would 'lose control', but was happy to keep at about 7 st 10 lb (49 kg).

At this time she moved to a city 125 miles away to run a restaurant, and began to write letters. Two months after her move she wrote:

Well, I weighed myself recently and I'm just 7 st 5 lb (47 kg). I'm not consciously trying to lose weight, but its obvious I'm not eating enough. I'm not missing out on any meals and eat a varied diet — including supposedly fattening foods. But my brain still ticks in the same way as before — that I'm not allowed to get fat. What's wrong with me? I can't go through life needing someone to reinforce the fact that I have to be at a higher weight before my hormones will start functioning. I still feel the need to be reassured that it's OK to be 8 st or 8½ st (52 or 54 kg) — whatever I'm supposed to be. Now it's only me, telling me I'm not allowed to get fat. I can't believe I'm so thick headed!

Two months later

One positive fact is that I haven't lost any weight. But how true that at a low weight, your moods are more erratic and depressed and mental functioning is impaired. I can't believe it — people keep telling me I don't eat enough but the whole day is 'a meal'. I can't stuff anymore into me. If my bowels would function normally maybe I would have more appetite. I've been more tense in the last 3 or 4 weeks, it upsets me terribly. The more depressed I become the less I want to be with people. I could quite happily exist alone — I'm constantly accusing myself of things and apologizing to other people. I talk to other people but do not listen to what they say. I know I must be a pain but I can't seem to do anything about it. I don't want to come back because I know I would run home to the family for protection — they'd assure me that everything was OK when I know damn well it isn't. I'm wasting my life — it is a chore just to get through the day. I want to come back and talk to you when I get my holidays later this year.

Three months after her last letter, Alison returned to the Clinic. She was neatly, even elegantly, dressed but looked thin. She weighed 7 st 3 lb

(46 kg). Over the next few months she increased her weight at the rate of 2 lb (1 kg) a month and has now maintained a body weight of 7 st 12 lb (50 kg) for the past two years. She has formed relationships and has a steady boyfriend. She continues to excel in her work as manager of a restaurant.

Most anorexia nervosa patients have a preoccupation with food and control of their weight. Food and its avoidance becomes an all-absorbing hobby to the exclusion of most of the other activities they would normally indulge in at their particular age, especially social occasions when food is usually present and eating expected. The preoccupation with weight is such that most patients can give a detailed history of their weight changes, including changes as small as 1 lb (0.5 kg), over periods as short as a week. The preoccupation about food and weight. control and the overwhelming urge to become thin, leads anorexia nervosa patients to use a range of eating behaviour to achieve their desire.

Young women whose weight has usually been in the normal range before their eating disorder began, generally lose weight by the simple method of eating less and by avoiding situations in which they have to eat. In order to avoid eating they make excuses such as 'I don't feel hungry at the moment so I'll eat some later', when told by parents that a meal is ready. They tend to avoid social occasions, often locking themselves in their room and asking not to be disturbed. They may be competitive and are often obsessive about their work, which enables them to avoid social occasions where food is eaten. In addition to strict dieting, they may use exercise as a method of losing weight. This may involve jogging, playing squash, attending 'health farms', or 'working out' at a gymnasium for long hours.

Case history: Jennifer

Jenny was 15 when she went on holiday on her own. At the sea-side resort she entered a beauty contest and came second. That night she got drunk for the first time, and had her first experience of sexual intercourse. She felt guilty about being drunk and about having sex. At school she was a good student, worked hard and excelled in sports, swimming, playing hockey, and basketball in the school team. On her return from holiday she believed that she would have won the beauty contest if she had been slimmer and if her thighs and bottom had been smaller. She decided to go on a diet to lose weight, and this resulted in arguments with her mother, who thought that Jennifer was already too thin.

Jenny compromised by offering to do the cooking (in reality it was to help her have control over the calorie content). During meals she moved the food about the plate so that she appeared to be eating. She avoided cream and fatty foods, telling her family that they made her feel sick. She spent long hours alone in her room studying and in the evenings attended dancing classes. In her room she exercised strenuously, for 15 to 20 minutes every two hours, and played music to hide the noise of her exercises from her parents. She told them that the music helped her concentration on her studies. She became obsessional about her weight, weighing herself before and after meals, before and after bouts of exercise, and before and after going to the toilet.

At about this time she was chosen to represent her state in a folk-dancing championship and increased her daily exercise, telling her parents that she had to be 'super fit to help my team win'. With increasing exercise and a limited food intake, Jennifer's weight dropped from 8 st 4 lb (53 kg) to 7 st (45 kg). She wore loose clothes to disguise her low weight from her family. However, one morning her mother saw her naked and was horrified. Jenny promised to eat more, but again managed to disguise the amount she ate and whenever possible slipped food from her plate to the family dog.

As the time of the folk dancing championships approached Jenny increased the amount of exercise she did daily, and because she still felt she was too fat, restricted her food intake still further. Two weeks before the championships she collapsed and was admitted to hospital. Her weight was now 4 st 10 lb (30 kg). In hospital she was given sedatives. She felt that she was no longer in control of her weight, she became agitated and was given additional medication. With refeeding she gained 17 lb (8 kg) and with her parents agreement discharged herself from hospital.

At home she continued to exercise excessively and again collapsed. She was readmitted to hospital and remained in hospital until her weight had increased to 8 st (49 kg) (90 per cent of Average Body Weight). During this hospital admission she agreed to and worked out a diet with the dietitian. Since discharge she has maintained her weight at around 7 st 10 lb (46 kg) (85 per cent of ABW). At first she was terrified that she would gain weight and began exercising again. This has become an obsession so much so that she jogs in the streets if her doctor is running late with his appointments. However, in spite of a strenuous exercise programme, she eats sufficient food to maintain her body weight.

The second group of anorexia nervosa patients, who have more often been overweight before the start of the illness, and whose weight

53

tends to fluctuate during the illness, use potentially dangerous methods to lose weight. In this behaviour they resemble binge-eaters. They usually deny that they have any concern about their weight. In public, or among the family, they may appear to eat normal amounts of food. However, having eaten, they make excuses to leave the group and induce vomiting, often combining this with the excessive use of laxatives. Because of their eating habits, phases of severe weight reduction, causing emaciation, are interspaced with periods of weight gain. They tend to be fairly social, and are less obsessional than the 'dieters'. In some cases, the woman has been a binge-eater for several months, or even years, before a decision to lose weight relentlessly precipitates her into anorexia nervosa.

Case history: Barbara

Barbara thinks that she began binge-eating when she was ten. The binge usually consisted of eating a packet or two of biscuits, several ice creams, and whatever she could find in the house when she came home from school. By the age of 13, Barbara weighed 11 st (70 kg) (143 per cent of Average Body Weight) and began to menstruate. A year later she became interested in boys, became aware that she was fat, and stopped eating sweets and cakes. She knew she was overweight but was popular and had an active social life. As she was intelligent she achieved high grades at school. Over the next five years her weight decreased slowly so that by the age of 18 she weighed 9 st 12 lb (63 kg). At this time problems in her parents' marriage were becoming apparent. She obtained entry to university and enjoyed the experience, but at the end of the second year, she decided that she must lose weight for the coming summer and began dieting. She also avoided eating whilst studying. As a result her weight fell to 8 st 13 lb (57 kg) over a period of four months. She restricted her diet further, began counting calories and started jogging. In addition she started taking laxatives daily because of constipation. Her parents had now separated and after trying to live with her father she moved into her mother's house. By winter her weight had dropped to 5 st (32 kg) and her periods had ceased. She abused laxatives and on days of overeating took emetics so that she would vomit afterwards. She was also able to obtain diuretics from the family doctor for her 'fluid retention'. With these medications, the dieting and the vomiting she became sufficiently ill to be admitted to hospital for refeeding. In hospital she lost control of her eating and ate everything she could obtain, with the result that her weight increased rapidly and she was praised by the staff. Her weight was now 6 st 10 lb (43 kg) (88 per cent of ABW) and she was discharged 'cured of anorexia nervosa'.

Her preoccupation with being extremely thin had ceased, but she still had an eating disorder. This became apparent later that year when she went to India with a group of students to visit Kashmir. She wrote to the clinic from there:

I spent the first 3 weeks of the holiday trekking in Kashmir which is astonishingly beautiful. I was enjoying the fantastic scenery, the fresh air, and the exercise and seemed to escape my problems up here high in the mountains. But on the last days of the trek, I got extremely sick with acute dysentery, fever — the works — and reached Srinagar in great distress doubled up by unbelievable cramps. I had to stay in bed for several weeks feeling pretty rotten. Four of my friends got hepatitis and the hospital was appalling. So what did I do? I ate, believe it or not! Few but ex(?) anorexics could eat with such gusto, in spite of abdominal pains, but somehow I managed and I have continued to eat since I came home. I am now even fatter than before — I'm 10 st 5 lb (66 kg) and still have diarrhoea and cramps at times. But these will go; the stool tests are negative. What I'm rather distressed about is my weight (what else!) as I feel it is slowly destroying my ability to cope with everyday life. Just as my eating behaviour is out of control, my life seems to be getting the same way. My social life is eventful and fun, on the whole, and I'm not withdrawn, but I have that frantic sense of imminent doom and I'm incredibly fearful of putting on more weight. I've tried many ways to overcome whatever it is that makes me eat but I can't break the pattern for more than 2 or 3 days. I've thought of the alternatives — getting fatter, vomiting, starving — even suicide . . . but actually I'd give my right arm to have the whole lot sorted out. I'm enjoying Uni, and the course which is full of interest (when I'm not occupying my mind with stagnant thoughts of weight and food). I'd rather anything than spending half my time (and all my money) on food. And it was this feeling that made me diet, and become anorexic, two years ago.

I am lying down listening to Mozart. I should be writing an essay but I ate so much yesterday that I have bad cramps plus an upper abdominal pain from eating too much today. Musing over how long it will take to lose 3 stone in the shortest quickest way — etcetera, etcetera — and it sure is a BLOODY WASTE of TIME. I've got a lovely family, some good friends, a fantastic boyfriend, lots of material assets — and instead I retreat into this *awful* life I've created for myself. Is it going to be like this forever? I couldn't stand it for much longer. I feel like it is moving in upon me and asphyxiating me.

I can't get much done at all as I'm so caught up in this 'vicious circle' — I'm just as obsessed with food as I was 2 years ago and I want to escape or it will be 3 years, 4 years — ad infinitum. An unbearable thought.

ANOREXIA NERVOSA IN MALES

Anorexia nervosa occurs in males fifteen times less frequently than in females. It begins in the same way and its course is similar. Most males with anorexia nervosa are compulsive exercisers, spending long hours each day jogging, doing press-ups, and other exercises. They are as obsessed about food as women but are less likely to show the same interest in cooking and cookbooks. Why males should pursue thinness so relentlessly is obscure, as adolescent men seek to be muscular rather than thin. Men who develop anorexia nervosa may also binge-eat; an example is John who explained why he binge-ate in a letter.

Whenever I get worried about the fact that I have anorexia nervosa and that I binge-eat as well (and I have to admit vomit after the binge) my thoughts turn to Uncle Harry and his character, personality, and his periods of depression. I don't know him too well so the following is only a theory but it seems to fit to our — his and my — personality traits and our mental histories. The theory came into my mind when I was talking to Bill about my eating problems; I don't talk to many people about them but I did to Bill. Bill said 'You set your standards pretty high'. He's right, of course, I do and it may explain my recent overconscientiousness and overconsciousness — an overconsciousness of myself which has trapped me in a small world of self so that I have found it hard to work, to study, to relax, to sleep, to concentrate or even to communicate with others. I have become overconscious of everything I say and do. So when Bill said 'you set your standards pretty high', at first I thought it sounded like flattery. But when I thought about it more I have realized that it may have some truth in it.

I have to admit that prior to moving here I had a method of relaxing and releasing this tension. I'd binge. Certainly I felt guilty as I was a strain and burden on Mum and Dad. Since moving I have tried to have as few binges as possible. In all fairness, I have cut down on binges. (I try not to keep count, but I must maintain this positive attitude.) However, regardless of any physical success I *may* have had, the mental impact of telling myself 'I can't' and 'I must not' or 'I intend to go the next three weeks without a single binge', creates much tension and depression. Remember, I no longer have 'bingeing' as an outlet for any 'natural' everyday type tensions. As a matter of fact, the desire to *stop* bingeing has become a tension-maker within itself.

The result is that my tension and depression builds to the point of desperation when I feel I am near insanity and even contemplate suicide. It never gets any further than this as (and I am sad to admit this, but it seems true) I end up having a binge. Somehow, I end up feeling more relaxed.

However, I then promise myself to make a more determined effort to beat the bingeing and the cycle starts again. This tension 'build-up' cycle not only applies to my bingeing. It also applies to other projects, plans, and aspects of my life. I seem to set a goal that *may* be just that little bit too high for me. I don't accept myself and my own limitations. I seem to set myself up for failure.

Everyone suffers tensions. Those who handle them best seem to have some way of relaxing. I *used* to have my bingeing. Although I still have binges *physically*, I now seem to have placed a *mental* prohibition on binges, the *mental* prohibition itself creates tension which sometimes causes a *physical* binge and thus not only becomes ineffective, but also becomes a causal factor itself.

In other words, I either have to find another method of relaxation or, at least for the time being, accept my human weaknesses and by this, I mean accept an at least limited amount of bingeing. Two important points: first, another form of relaxation will probably have to come about naturally. I don't think I will be able to consciously search for one. If I try to search for one the mere fact that I am conscious of it can prevent relaxation. Second, I find it hard to mentally accept a limited amount of bingeing in the future. Both because I have become determined to defeat it (once again setting my goal too high??) and because of my insecurity, especially financially, as I no longer live with Mum and Dad. Although Mum and Dad have assured me that they would always help me (and I believe trust and love them) there is a large physical distance between us. I also fear that if I let up my 'guard' against bingeing to allow 'limited' bingeing (by limited I mean once, maybe twice, a week), I may end up slipping back and bingeing more. Would Mum and Dad help me then?? . . .

Anyway, I digress. Uncle Harry is a person who sets high standards for himself. I don't feel I'm guessing. He's achieved a hell of a lot in his life; but instead of being proud of it, he is only ashamed/guilty (for the want of better words) for what he hasn't achieved. Look!! He played first class cricket, he's been a successful headmaster. He's had a success-ful family life (many don't these days) and he's raised three healthy, intelligent and successful children. He's been superannuated and is just as well off as he was when he worked. (This might not be a fantastic achievement, but how many people can retire at 50 yrs. with the prospect of leading a secure, fulfilling and useful life). Me, I haven't achieved any of these things (and actually don't seem to have achieved much), except being thin.

Anyway, the key to Uncle Harry's and my problems is *tension!!* This tension isn't caused by external factors (such as family, work or social problems) but internal standards we set ourselves. I seem to continually set myself up to fail by setting goals that are not within my reach (at least in the time span I allow and expect). It is probably about time we accept our own weaknesses (food may be mine but I'll never admit or accept it??) our inevitable failing, our limitations and the limits of the human body and mind. We can only do our best and unfortunately our best may sometimes be less than what we, ourselves, expect. Don't worry about whether other people accept us — if they can't accept us as we are with our limitations, that's *their* problem, *not* ours. . .

Uncle Harry's and my basic problem is the self-inflicted tensions we impose on ourselves. In the past, I have used bingeing to relieve my tensions. I sometimes fear I may suffer nervous breakdowns if I can't find a way to relax. Just lately, especially with my at least attempted mental (if not physical) non-acceptance of bingeing, my fears of having some sort of breakdown have been far from a fantasy. Anyway, the answer for Uncle Harry and me may be this: *accept* ourselves for what we are; *accept* our limitations. For Uncle Harry this may be accepting that he was not meant to be some of the things he feels he should have been or had a duty to be or do. For me, this may mean accepting (and I still don't want to admit it) bingeing to a small extent while I allow some other element to replace it naturally (but by God, I'll still search hard and experiment until I find this other element).

I also have a great need for affiliation, friendship, love and a need to feel needed. But as I said, if others can't accept us as we are, that's *their* problem. There will always be someone to accept us as we are (these people are friends worthy of having).

If we accept ourselves, we can relax. Tension and our own inner self-competitiveness will float away. We can then concentrate on gifting to others and the world, those good points we have *AND EVERYBODY* (no matter who they are) has good points!! *EVERYBODY!!!*

[handwritten: Lots of insight but lack of abstinence. self-help group]

THE ONSET OF ANOREXIA NERVOSA

Anyway, when I first started to diet I set myself a specific amount that I was allowed to eat each day — usually birdlike portions. I would suffer endlessly if my plan was disrupted by an invitation to lunch. To eat a large meal in the middle of the day was a source of a most guilty conscience for days after, that was the extent of my paranoia! I stuck to my diet religiously. But my reward was always a Coconut Honey Log on Friday afternoons, and, I allowed myself to eat bread during the weekend.

The decision to diet in order to become thin is triggered in a variety of ways, depending on the woman's personality and the particular circumstances in which she finds herself. Often the onset of anorexia nervosa in a young girl follows an awareness that she does not like the shape or size of her body. As has been mentioned, concern about body shape and size is common among adolescent girls; but in the case of those who have anorexia nervosa, it becomes an obsession. The young woman's preoccupation with her body and her weight often follows a challenge, for example, her family or her friends may tease her about her shape and her weight; or it may follow a competition with a friend to lose weight. Family stress may be a factor of considerable importance in triggering the onset of anorexia. The most common factor is an independence/dependence struggle between the young woman and one or both parents, who give mixed messages, for example, 'you must be independent but we need you at home'. In other cases the young woman is confused: wanting to be independent yet dependent. For example, she may say 'I want to do things my way but I want the security of home'. In other instances the onset of anorexia is associated with a series of events which are stressful in themselves, such as a break-up with a boyfriend, the first experience of sexual intercourse, an unwanted pregnancy, marriage, a major examination, or with a period of further deterioration in already stressful circumstances such as parents separating; or increasing pressure on the girl to 'achieve' at school or in extracurricular activities such as sport or dancing.

THE PHYSICAL FEATURES OF ANOREXIA NERVOSA

Before I started to lose weight I weighed about 8 st 3 lb (52 kg) and had reached my present height. Common sense tells me that my weight was not heavy for that height. But common sense had left me and I wanted to weigh about 95 lbs (43 kg). And I achieved it! The strange

thing is that whenever I went to buy new clothes I always saw how revoltingly thin my image in the mirror actually was. But I still felt fat.

The physical symptoms of the illness may result from the behaviour which the girl has used to achieve a loss in weight or from her low body weight itself. When a woman becomes emaciated, her insulating layer of fat is largely lost and in consequence she becomes sensitive to hot and cold temperatures; her hands and feet feel cold and often look blue; her skin may become dry; her hair brittle, and a soft downy hair, called lanugo, may appear on her face, back, or arms. Her heart rate slows down, and her blood pressure falls, probably because her body tries to adjust to the low energy intake by using less energy. In spite of this, the response of patients suffering from anorexia nervosa to exercise is normal and their heart rate increases to the same extent as that of 'normal' women. The bowel motility of many anorexia nervosa patients diminishes because there is less food in the intestines to stimulate peristaltic activity, and constipation is usual. If the woman has been on a starvation diet she may develop a vitamin deficiency which can be quite severe.

Case history: Sandra

Sandra was a tall, quiet girl who was considerate, competent and well-liked at school. In consequence she was given responsibility both at school and at home.

When she was 14 years old, her weight was 10 st 7 lb (67 kg) 107 per cent of Average Body Weight). She felt that she was too fat and decided to lose weight. Her elder sister had been told by a modelling school that one way was to induce vomiting by putting a finger down her throat. Sandra decided to do this but was disappointed that little weight loss occurred so she accepted her existing weight as normal and ceased to worry about it. She began swimming competitively and by the age of 17 felt fit, competent, confident, and had lost 13 lb (6 kg).

Her eighteenth year was one of tragedy. Her mother was killed in a car accident, leaving two younger children. Her older sister became a drug addict and Sandra injured herself so that she had to give up swimming. She felt she could no longer cope and deferred taking her higher school certificate for a year. Sandra took over the responsibilities of housekeeper and looked after her younger sisters. During this period her feeling of confidence and competency disappeared. She wrote in her diary:

and I know what I should be doing! Going out and meeting people is a major effort and hassle for me but I feel so uncomfortable and inadept in company, especially in arranging to go to new places and meet new people that I end up settling for my own company. Food and eating has become such an integral part of everything. I don't want to be like this but what I eat rules my life so that every waking minute seems occupied with thoughts of food and the day passes in the measured times between when I last ate and when I'll eat again. I dream of the perfect day when I have no appetite and no thought, desire or temptation for food or to eat.

When she was 19 she returned to complete her higher school certificate at the local technical college, where comments about her 'emaciation' induced her to eat more. Increasing her food intake was associated with episodes of binge-eating which alarmed her. She began to induce vomiting (remembering her sister's advice) by putting her fingers down her throat. Soon she was inducing vomiting up to ten times a day. It became increasingly difficult to dispose of the vomit. She resorted to vomiting into plastic bags and disposing these in the garbage bin. Her father found out what she was doing and insisted that she visit a doctor who made a diagnosis of anorexia nervosa, as her weight was 6 st. 2 lb (39 kg) He arranged for her to be admitted to hospital to help her gain weight and to stop her vomiting. In hospital she was co-operative and liked by the staff. A psychiatric consultation showed no major psychiatric illness. She was able to continue studying while in hospital and after discharge sat for and passed the examination. Her weight was now 7 st 3 lb (46 kg). She persisted in dieting and in self-induced vomiting and became weak. This induced her to seek re-admission to hospital. Blood studies showed that the vomiting had caused a low blood potassium. She was treated with potassium supplement and an intravenous infusion.

Over the next three years during a university course she had six re-admissions to hospital for the effects of low body potassium, including impending renal failure and heart-beat problems (arrhythmias). The admissions followed periods of increased binge-eating and vomiting which Sandra related to stress from family problems. She battled against treatment saying that her illness was 'all my fault because I will go on vomiting' and resolved each day to stop. But each day she broke her resolution when she panicked about becoming fat and when she ate food. Although she was watched by her family she managed to dispose of her vomit by hiding it in the garden or in plastic bags which she took to the university where she disposed of it. Sandra's illness became the scapegoat for the family's problems which were considerable.

Her father remarried during this time and on obtaining her degree Sandra left home. Over the next three years her weight increased slowly

Eating disorders — the facts

and is now 8 st 6 lb (53.9 kg). She no longer induces vomiting. When last contacted she said 'I look back in horror and wonder if it was some terrible nightmare.'

Behaviour aimed at achieving weight loss, such as self-induced vomiting and the abuse of laxatives and diuretics also cause physical disturbances, and may lead to an electrolyte disturbance, initially due to loss of

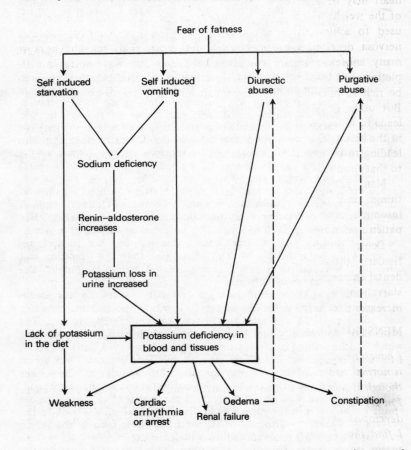

Fig. 11. Electrolyte problems in anorexia nervosa

potassium. The low body (and tissue) potassium causes impairment of neuromuscular function, which results in weakness and tingling in the hands and feet. Other symptoms include lassitude, emotional lability (violent swings in mood), and intestinal dilation, which gives a feeling of extreme bloating and aggravates the constipation. Some patients find that they bruise easily. In severe cases of potassium deficiency the heart may be affected or paralysis may occur. In spite of the severity of the weight loss and the potentially dangerous nature of the methods used to achieve it, it is surprising how few patients with anorexia nervosa develop severe potassium deficiency. This may be because many anorexics realize that their behaviour can cause potassium depletion, and take supplements of potassium or eat foods they know to be rich in potassium (such as tomatoes, capsicum, and orange juice). But other physiological explanations are possible. The vomiting also leads to a degree of alkalosis and to a fall in ionized calcium circulating in the blood. The low level of ionized calcium may cause muscle spasms leading to twitching of muscles and involuntary hand clenching, similar to that found in tetany.

Many patients suffering from anorexia are hyperactive, always doing things, and unable to relax. The hyperactivity may be the cause of insomnia, especially early morning waking, which is a feature in some patients with anorexia nervosa.

Dental problems also occur among anorexia nervosa patients, particularly those who induce vomiting. The main problem is a loss of dental enamel, due to the effects of acid vomit on the teeth. In addition, starvation, by altering the quantity and composition of the saliva, increases the likelihood of dental decay.

MENSTRUAL DISTURBANCES IN ANOREXIA NERVOSA

I haven't had my periods for the last 10 years. I have forgotten that it is normal to have periods – and not normal to be without them. Even though it seems a lot easier and convenient for them to be non-existent, I'm also aware that I'm not experiencing the emotional state of a fully developed woman because of the shut-down of my hormonal system. I find that I am feeling deprived of this privilege but the only way to regain my periods, is to do the positive thing that will remedy this situation – eat!

A major physical problem among females ill with anorexia nervosa is that they fail to reach menarche, or their menstrual periods cease, often before much weight has been lost. Indeed, the absence of menstruation (amenorrhoea) is one of the features essential for a diagnosis to be made.

The explanation of the menstrual disturbances is rather complex, as it involves the interplay of a number of hormones. The control of these hormonal relationships is situated in the area of the brain called the hypothalamus, which in turn is influenced by messages from other parts of the brain, and from outside, such as an emotional shock.

In childhood, before puberty, throughout the reproductive years and into old age the hypothalamus secretes and releases several hormones into small blood-vessels which carry them to the pituitary gland where they induce the synthesis and release of pituitary hormones, which have profound effects on the body. Because they cause the pituitary gland to release hormones, the hormones made in the hypothalamus are called releasing hormones.

. The releasing hormone concerned with ovulation and menstruation is called the gonadotrophic-releasing hormone or GnRH. In childhood, a small but constant amount of GnRH is released, but in the years just prior to the onset of menstruation, a change occurs and GnRH begins to be released in pulsatile surges throughout the day. These pulsatile surges begin when the girl begins to grow rather rapidly in the three or four years before menarche. When her body reaches a 'critical' weight, or more accurately when the proportion of fat in her body exceeds a critical level, she menstruates for the first time, reaching menarche. Once menarche has been reached, GnRH continues to be released in a pulsatile manner throughout the reproductive years, the quantity varying from day to day. For example during menstruation a large surge of GnRH occurs and this stimulates specialized cells in the pituitary gland to synthesize and to release follicle-stimulating hormone (or FSH). As its name implies, FSH stimulates the growth of a number of egg-containing structures (follicles) in the ovary. At puberty each ovary contains over 200 000 follicles. Each month between puberty and menopause, 10 to 20 follicles are stimulated to grow; one of them outstripping all the others. As they develop, they synthesize the female sex hormone, oestrogen, and release it into the circulating blood. Oestrogen

Anorexia nervosa

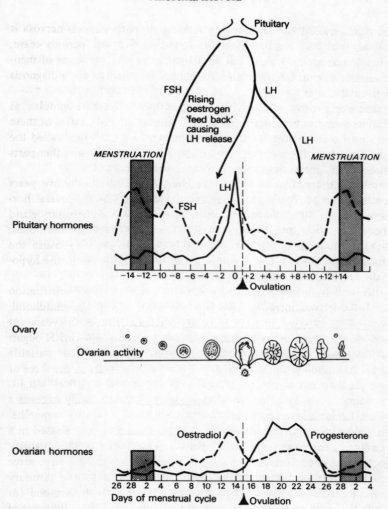

Fig. 12. The control of menstruation

is taken up preferentially by the tissues of the genital organs and the breasts, particularly by the glandular lining, or endometrium of the uterus and that of the breasts which are induced to develop, increasing in thickness. At the same time the rising amounts of oestrogen in the blood 'feed back negatively' to the hypothalamus and to the pituitary gland, leading to a slow fall in the amount of GnRh released and consequently a fall in FSH. At midcycle, that is about 16 days before the next menstrual period, a surge of oestrogen secretion occurs, causing a 'positive feedback' to the hypothalamus and to the pituitary. In response the pituitary releases both a surge of FSH and a surge of a second hormone, the luteinizing hormone or LH. LH, in turn, acts on the largest of the growing follicles, which is three times as large as all the others, measuring about 23 mm. The follicle, by this time, has stretched the surface of the ovary. The follicle 'bursts' and releases its ovum (or egg). Ovulation has occurred. LH also causes changes in the character of the collapsed follicle, now called a 'corpus luteum'. It becomes yellow and begins to synthesize and release a second female sex hormone, progesterone. Progesterone develops the endometrium further, so that it is ready should the ovum be fertilized. If fertilization fails to occur, the corpus luteum dies, and ceases to produce hormones. This leads to menstruation and a repetition of the hormonal cycle.

It has been observed that the close interrelationships of the hormones can be interrupted by a number of factors. If the body weight falls below a critical level, the hypothalamus fails to release GnRH in pulsatile surges. In consequence, the pituitary fails to release sufficient FSH to stimulate the ovaries, and menstruation ceases. Once the body weight increases above the critical level, the menses resume, often after a delay. It is also known that excessive exercise inhibits pulsatile GnRH release with consequent amenorrhoea. A woman whose weight is below normal, but above the critical level, and who exercises excessively, for example a ballet dancer, also fails to menstruate, becoming amenorrhoeic.

The hormonal changes discussed provide an explanation for the menstrual disturbances. When a woman's Quetelet index (see p. 15) falls to 15 or below, or her body weight falls below the critical level of approximately 80 per cent of the Average Body Weight, GnRH ceases to be released in a pulsatile manner, and the surges of GnRH are replaced by a steady low secretion, similar to that which occurred before puberty. Because GnRH is no longer released in surges, the pituitary fails to release FSH and LH at levels sufficient to stimulate the ovaries to secrete sufficient amounts of the female sex hormones and amenorrhoea results.

It is interesting that between 10 and 20 per cent of anorexia nervosa patients develop amenorrhoea before any weight loss has occurred (in fact their weight may even be increasing) and others do not resume regular menses for some months or years after return to normal body weights. If a detailed history is taken from these women it is usually found that they have been using weight-losing methods such as excessive exercise, self-induced vomiting, and laxative abuse before weight loss or during and after weight gain. In these cases the menstrual disturbance is almost certainly associated with the weight-losing behaviour.

However, not all patients who continue to have amenorrhoea before they have lost much weight, or after refeeding, use such methods, so that some other explanation is possible. At present we do not know what it is.

Case history: Maria

Maria is the attractive youngest daughter of a family who emigrated to Australia before she was born. At the age of 14, a year after her menstrual periods started she became aware that her family were fat, and she did not want to become fat like them. Her weight was within the desirable range at 7 st 6 lb (47.5 kg) (100 per cent of Average Body Weight) and she was teased at school as being a 'sexy Italian'. She bought some slimming tablets from the chemist, but after taking them for 5 days stopped because they 'did no good'. As her friends at school were dieting, she decided to do so, too. Her plan was to eat normally for one day and starve the next day. She tended to overeat when not starving so that after two months she had gained, not lost, 8 lb (4 kg). She heard that if she took laxatives she would lose weight, and as her mother had put out laxatives for the family when they had not opened their bowels each day, felt she had 'permission' to use laxatives to lose weight. She also started exercising, spending 1 or 2 hours a day in exercise, telling the family she was preparing for the school sports.

Within a month of starting the exercise programme, her menstrual periods ceased although she had only lost 4 lb (1.8 kg). Maria was secretly pleased that she had no periods but was worried that people might know and wonder if she was normal. For the next five months in spite of exercise and laxatives her weight remained the same. In desperation to lose weight Maria refused to eat with the family as the food was 'all pasta and unhealthy'. By the age of 16, she was dieting rigidly and was abusing laxatives. Her weight began to decrease and on her

18th birthday she weighed 4 st 12 lb (31 kg) (65 per cent of ABW). Her parents now intervened. She was admitted to hospital with a diagnosis of anorexia nervosa and started on a refeeding programme.

After three months when she was discharged from hospital her weight had increased to 7 st (45 kg) (95 per cent of ABW) and she had a menstrual period. At home, she continued to be afraid of becoming fat and returned to using excessive laxatives and dieted carefully to maintain her weight at about 7 st. She had no further menstrual periods until a year later when she found a job and a boyfriend of whom her parents approved. She started menstruating in spite of the fact that her weight had fallen to 6 st 8 lb (42 kg).

THE DIET OF ANOREXIA NERVOSA PATIENTS

As has been mentioned earlier, anorexia nervosa patients are preoccupied with food. They collect and read books and magazine articles relating to food, dieting, and body weight. Often they take over cooking for the family. They have a better knowledge of nutrition than the general public. Several investigators have shown that many women who have anorexia nervosa avoid carbohydrates in their diet, and that a low carbohydrate intake is the distinctive feature of the diet chosen so that they will lose weight. However a recent study in Sydney places some doubt on whether 'carbohydrate starvation' is the distinctive feature of anorexia nervosa. Seventeen patients who had been ill with anorexia nervosa for less than 15 months volunteered to be interviewed by a dietitian on two occasions: from these interviews typical daily food intakes were reconstructed, and the diet eaten by the women at the peak of their illness was compared with that of 'normal' women of similar age. The diet of a patient with anorexia nervosa contained one-sixth the energy, one-sixth the carbohydrate, one-third the protein and one-ninth the fat of a normal woman's diet. When the proportion of energy obtained from carbohydrate, protein, and fat was calculated, the amount obtained from carbohydrate was similar in both groups. This indicates that the anorexia nervosa patients reduced all items of their weight-losing diet and did not preferentially starve themselves of carbohydrate. These findings suggest that they have a better than average knowledge of nutrition, but these women, although scoring higher in a test of nutritional knowledge as a group, showed wide individual variations.

THE TREATMENT OF ANOREXIA NERVOSA

Its about time I got over my anorexia, and I agree that I've wasted enough time on it. But at times I think that I hang on to my old patterns of eating behaviour, or really non-eating behaviour, as the only secure thing I can fashion from such a changing and, as I feel sometimes, topsy turvey life. I often feel that this is the only part of my life over which I can exercise any sort of control, though it ends up in the absurdity of feeling that every bite is an act of losing control.

Before any treatment is offered, the doctor must have taken a careful history to confirm that the woman has anorexia nervosa and not that her body weight is low as a consequence of experimenting with dieting, her choice of a career, or her life-style.

An example of the importance of making this distinction is that of Zoe.

Zoe had always wanted to be a ballet dancer, and at the age of 15 was selected by her ballet teacher to compete for a place in a prestigous full-time ballet school. Her teacher had impressed on her the need to be thin and had weighed her once a week from the age of 12, praising her for keeping thin. Zoe said she had never had to control her weight consciously as she went to ballet classes three evenings each week, and didn't eat between school and the class. When she was weighed six months before the selection process her ballet teacher told her that she would have to lose some weight or she would not be selected. At that time her Quetelet Index was 17.5 and her weight was 85 per cent of the Average Body Weight.

She started dieting and soon her weight loss was noticed by the headmistress of her school who contacted Zoe's mother fearing that Zoe was another girl who had anorexia nervosa. Her mother at once took Zoe to a doctor who arranged for her to be admitted to hospital for refeeding. Her Quetelet Index was now 16 (78 per cent Average Body Weight). In hospital she refused to eat, or gave her food to other patients. She adopted this strategy because she believed that if she gained weight her chance of selection to the ballet school would be jeopardized. Her resistance to refeeding confirmed to the health professionals that Zoe had anorexia nervosa. She was also considered by them to be uncooperative, untruthful, and difficult.

After three weeks in hospital she had failed to gain any weight, and after discussion was taken home by her parents. She was then referred to one of us. When we talked with Zoe, her fear of not being selected for the ballet school became clear. We reassured her that in Australia, ballet dancers needed to have a Quetelet Index of at least 18 (80 to 90 per cent of Average Body Weight), or they would 'not look good on stage'. Zoe accepted the reassurance and gained 5 lb 8 oz (2.5 kg) in the next five weeks, which brought her weight into the desired range.

She was selected to train at the ballet school and has maintained her weight within the range acceptable for a dancer since that time. She does not appear to be more preoccupied about food, dieting, or her weight than the other students, and is enjoying the training at which she has been very successful.

The reverse situation to that of Zoe can also occur, when the diagnosis of anorexia nervosa may be difficult as many young women who have the disorder initially deny their illness.

Anorexia nervosa is a psychological illness, during which physical symptoms may develop because of the self-induced starvation and other methods of inducing weight-loss. The main treatment is psychological, involving supportive psychotherapy, counselling about eating and potentially dangerous methods of losing weight, and, when appropriate, other psychological supports, such as relaxation, family therapy, and marital therapy.

In the past many treatments for anorexia nervosa have been suggested and used, such as insulin shock therapy, force-feeding, tube-feeding, 'sleep therapy', and using medications to stimulate appetite. These treatments are still being used and the results are presented at various conferences. It is true that they may work and the patient may put on weight while she is in hospital, but in no case has a follow-up period of over 12 months been reported. These treatments should not be used as they do not allow patients to learn or relearn normal eating behaviour and they often cause feelings of loss of control, and panic. Drugs are seldom necessary but they may be needed in certain cases, for example if a patient is clinically depressed she may need antidepressants or if she has an infection she may need antibiotics.

Anorexia nervosa patients are individuals. They have different problems, different needs, and are at different stages of their illness when they come for treatment — they need treatment by a person who can offer sympathetic understanding and individual treatment. This can be done by a multidisciplinary team as long as there is one consistent person in the team to whom the patient can relate and who can co-ordinate treatment.

The varied needs of the anorexic frequently call for a multidisciplinary approach, including help from a dietitian or a social worker. The time being spent with an individual health professional depends on the patient's current needs and the relationships formed — for example, the dietitian may be the main therapist in certain cases.

The principal problem in treatment is that the patient wants to eat but is terrified that if she does so she will lose control of her eating and be unable to limit her weight gain. For this reason the hope expressed by parents, partner, or friends of an anorexia nervosa victim that 'All she has to do to get better is to eat' is unrealistic and counterproductive. The fear of losing control often extends to other aspects of the patient's life, but is particularly relevant to body weight and to food intake. For example, the fear of losing control over body weight prevents the patient from eating more than the amount she has set herself as she believes that if she eats what 'other people eat' she will put on weight rapidly. Because of this fear, patients weigh themselves daily or more often, and if they find that they have gained 2 lb (1 kg) for no apparent reason, immediately restrict the amount of food they eat or use some other method of losing weight. Even when they are emaciated they often find it safer to underestimate the amount of food they eat, rather than risk losing control over eating. As anorexia nervosa patients love food, this need to control their food intake may cause psychological turbulence. They are fearful that if they permit themselves to eat, they may be unable to stop, and that they will go on an eating binge. As many have experienced binge-eating before and after developing anorexia nervosa, the fear is real to them and it requires considerable patience by the therapist to dispell it. The therapist must be aware, constantly, that treatment has three objectives.

The first is to help the patient increase her weight so that it is within the normal range, although it is on the thin side of normal (preferably about 90 per cent of average body weight, or a Quetelet Index of about 19). The reason for choosing this weight is that most physiological functions, such as temperature control and menstruation, will have returned or will soon return to normal at this weight. The weight level is also realistic as it helps the patient avoid feeling anxious about

71

becoming fat. The second objective is to help the patient learn to re-establish normal eating behaviour and to avoid other methods such as excessive exercise, self-induced vomiting, or laxative abuse. The third objective is to explain the physical symptoms in a way which is understood by the patient.

Increasing body weight

It is important for the patient to realize that the long-term aim is for her to learn to increase her weight and to maintain it within the normal desirable range for her age and height. This does not mean that she has to control her weight to within 1 lb (0.5 kg) on a day-to-day basis. In fact, weighing more than once a week is meaningless (unless the woman is in hospital receiving treatment) as it is normal for the weight to vary by more than 2 lb (1 kg) over a period of days. Although a weight of 90 per cent of average body weight is set as a target weight, this is the minimum weight for normal physiological function such as the return of menstruation. At this weight, the patient is still on the thin side of normal and as many women look better at a higher weight she may be encouraged to attempt this. There are certain exceptions. For example if the woman is a fashion model or a ballet dancer she may not accept a weight of 90 per cent of average body weight as desirable, and she and her therapist have to agree that a lower weight is appropriate in her case. They may also have to agree that she is likely to remain preoccupied with her weight and to limit her food intake, so that she may retain the body shape expected of her profession.

Weight gain is achieved by 'refeeding'. During refeeding the patient learns that as she gains weight, she will feel physically better and will be better able to cope with her everyday problems.

Weight gain may take place as an out-patient or admission to hospital may be necessary, or preferred by the patient. Out-patient treatment is appropriate for some patients. The advantages are that as an out-patient the patient can increase her weight at her own speed, so that she feels safe and in control; she has to take responsibility for her eating and, with support and guidance from the therapist, can relearn eating patterns which are appropriate to her life-style. Some women may be helped if she and her therapist agree that she may remain at the same weight for some weeks, before a further increase in weight is attempted.

This strategy helps the patient to gain confidence that she is in control. With her therapist's support and encouragement she learns how much she needs to eat to control her weight at an appropriate level. She has to be made aware that she will not be rewarded for gaining weight rapidly, as this may merely indicate that she is binge-eating.

The therapist also has the responsibility of helping the patient to adjust to the other problems (such as relationship problems) which may have arisen because of the patient's fear of losing control.

The therapist's function is to explore these problems with the patient, and to encourage her motivation to return to 'normal' eating. She must also give the patient the confidence to continue with treatment, and to learn to maintain her body weight within the normal range.

As the therapist becomes aware of the patient's fear of losing control and her resistance to changing her eating behaviour, it may become apparent that treatment will have to be delayed until the patient is 'ready to get better', even though this means that a few patients will become severely ill and have to be rescued from impending death by urgent admission to hospital. Other patients who require admission include those who are severely ill when first seen, those who fail to make progress as an out-patient, those who are found to continue with their weight-losing behaviour, and those who are incapable of responding to treatment as a result of the physical and mental consequences of the very low body weight. In other cases the patient's doctor may feel she should be admitted to hospital or she herself may prefer to be treated in hospital.

Hospital provides a supportive environment in which the patient can feel safe because she is able to avoid the problems and pressures of everyday life. In some cases she may have to be observed continually or kept in somewhat extreme isolation in a single-bedded room and have to stay in bed until the 'target weight' is reached by refeeding. This strategy is necessary because many patients try to find methods to avoid eating (by disposing of food in the w.c., or wash basin, or elsewhere); or getting rid of food by inducing vomiting or abusing laxatives.

During refeeding the patient is expected to eat a diet containing about 10.9 MJ to 12.5 MJ (2600–3000 Kcals) of energy each day. The diet is also devised to contain an adequate amount of carbohydrate so that the metabolic problem of ketosis is avoided. Such a diet, if followed, will lead to a weight gain of 1–4 lb (0.4–0.8 kg) per week. During re-feeding she is also taught to avoid using weight-losing behaviour.

If she eats the amount of food expected and conforms to treatment by avoiding weight-losing strategies, and starts gaining weight, she is offered a 'reward' or a 'privilege'. For example, she may be allowed to get up and have a shower, or to watch television. On the other hand, if she fails to put on weight she knows that privileges may be taken away and she may be ordered to go back to bed and stay there. Most authorities insist that the patient is weighed each day at the same time of day on the same scales, but some believe that because minor daily changes in weight occur, it is preferable to weigh the patient twice a week, not daily. Weighing has to be done to a ritual and the nurse has to make sure that the patient doesn't cheat, for example by putting weights in her pockets or by drinking a large amount of water just before being weighed.

During the time that she gains weight, the patient often feels 'full' and her stomach may bulge. She needs to be told that this will happen, and needs to be reassured that the abdominal swelling will not remain. Unless this is done, she may feel that she is losing control. These are temporary symptoms which the patient has to suffer to achieve her goal. The abdominal swelling is due to distension of the intestines, and once intestinal function becomes normal, the abdomen becomes flat, whilst fat is deposited on her limbs and body. During refeeding the patient should avoid buying tight-fitting clothes, such as jeans, because within two or three weeks after her desirable weight has been achieved and the distention has subsided, they will be too big. The appearance of a 'bulging stomach' is usually more marked among patients who are refed in hospital than among out-patients, when exercise may help in increasing intestinal tone and redistributing the weight gain.

When a reasonable amount of weight gain each week has been obtained, it will be found that the amount tapers off as the 'desirable' body weight is approached. At this stage women who are patients in hospital receive greater privileges but should remain in hospital for two weeks after their desirable body weight has been achieved to make sure that their weight is maintained and that they receive reinforcement that they have their weight under control and learn how much to eat.

74

Anorexia nervosa

Some patients say that when they are in control of their food intake and their body weight, they feel in control of their lives. For example, when preparing for an examination the patient may feel it would be 'good' to put on weight but resists this because if she starts to lose control of her eating behaviour she fears that she will lose control of her self discipline, will not study, and will fail the examination. Her control of her eating behaviour may continue for other reasons. It may become part of a reward–punishment system. She may argue: 'If I eat one extra thing, something dreadful will happen to me'. It may be used to manipulate parents or her husband, to gain attention, or as an excuse if she does not perform as well as they expect: 'If I am thin, people know there is something wrong and do not expect as much.'

Establishing normal eating behaviour

The second aim of treatment is for the patient to learn to eat sensibly, and to choose a nutritious diet rather than eating 'rubbish foods', or going on eating-binges. Eating sensibly includes learning to eat in social situations, and to be comfortable about this. For example, if someone who has had anorexia nervosa goes to a social function, such as a wedding or a Chinese banquet, she may eat far more than her body requires that day and has to learn that to accept that this is normal. She also has to conquer her preoccupation with food and her urge to weigh every item of food she eats, and to calculate its calorie content. Many patients have no idea of how much they can eat without weight gain and have trouble recognizing cues for hunger and satiation. During treatment they learn to recognize these cues and are taught the elements of dietetics.

A major concern is to change the potentially dangerous weight-losing behaviour resorted to by many women who have anorexia nervosa. Many patients respond to information about the short- and long-term effects of vomiting and abuse of purgatives, diuretics, and slimming-tablets, and are willing, at least initially, to reduce the frequency of these behaviours. They find reassurance on learning what effects to expect when they stop vomiting and using laxatives, for example, that they may undergo a temporary weight gain as they become rehydrated, and that constipation may persist for some time, as well as abdominal fullness and cramps. As the patients are preoccupied with body weight and abdominal fullness, these are the very symptoms which make them anxious and may make them return to vomiting and laxatives unless they know that these symptoms are to be expected.

Women who have anorexia nervosa may be manipulative and untruthful when they are questioned about their food intake or their methods of losing weight. The therapist may have to confront the patient before treatment is started, to establish, as far as possible, whether she is prepared to agree to try and eat more food. Truthful common-sense confrontation is also required during treatment if the patient is discovered cheating. For example, she may appear to take all the food offered and then dispose of most of it surreptitiously down the sink, or place weights in the pockets of her dressing gown when she knows that she is to be weighed. She may also secretly resort to self-induced vomiting or abuse laxatives when she decides that she has reached a certain weight and does not want to gain more, as she is fearful that she is losing control of her eating.

Explaining the physical symptoms

Some patients are content that they no longer menstruate, but if they are in their late teens or twenties they may need reassurance that menstruation will return if they maintain their higher weight, although it may be delayed for several months. As the patient gains weight she may want her menstrual periods to start again as she sees this as a demonstration that she is getting better. Other women require discussion and reassurance that their dry skin, broken hair, and lanugo hair will disappear as their nutrition improves. Pregnancy, which may occur during the recovery period, may pose considerable problems, particularly if the woman continues to use the potentially dangerous behaviours of self-induced vomiting, or laxative or diuretic abuse. The problems can be minimized by good prenatal care.

THE OUTCOME OF ANOREXIA NERVOSA

The aims of treatment are, first, to induce the woman to achieve and maintain a normal body weight, that is a weight lying between 90 and 110 per cent of the Average Body Weight for her age and height (or a Quetelet Index of 19 or more); secondly, to enable her to avoid potentially dangerous eating behaviour, and thirdly for her to perceive that she need have no fear of becoming obese, provided she pays attention to her eating habits.

About 70 per cent of anorexic patients achieve these aims after therapy lasting from six months to six years, but many need continuing counselling, particularly when they encounter stressful situations. The support from a therapist over a period of years may be necessary.

Kylie's story typifies the problem. In the previous three years she had had four admissions to hospital for refeeding. Each admission had lasted for at least two months. After being discharged from hospital for the fourth time she wrote to her doctor:

I know that I still look too thin, but I just don't seem able to regain the weight I lost in the last four months. It may be because I left home then. I was very worried about how I'd cope when I started living away from home again, and tried to be strict with myself about 'cutting back' on food. I don't think I did 'cut back', but suppose I'm a lot more active now at work than I was when I was at home leading a life of (enforced) leisure. However, I find it almost impossible to let myself eat more. As you may remember, my problem has always been an 'eating-food' one, rather than a concern with weight. Basically I still think the same way as I have for a long time, and I don't suppose this will ever change now.

Anorexia now seems to be becoming increasingly common, and receiving a lot of publicity. I don't know whether the publicity is all for the good — I have the feeling it may be becoming almost 'fashionable' among young girls, without their realising its long-term consequences. If I could but turn the clock back about twelve years; wishful thinking!

A year later, Kylie wrote again:

Considering everything I've been keeping quite well. I've maintained my weight since I left the Clinic (over a year ago now!) though I haven't put any more on. I'm still not over-confident about how I would cope on my own, i.e. if I was preparing and responsible for all my own food. So many of the old attitudes are still lying dormant and I have to be ever vigilant that they don't exert too much influence. All in all its still not terribly easy, though I must admit that I do think less and less about being an 'anorexic'.

Between 15 and 25 per cent of anorexia nervosa patients, mainly those whose eating behaviour includes binge-eating, self-induced vomiting, and purging continue to binge-eat intermittently, and may need help to overcome this.

The remaining 10 to 20 per cent of anorexia nervosa patients continue to be ill with anorexia nervosa, requiring intermittent therapy over many years. The last two groups of patients require the support of, and to be counselled by, a therapist at intervals for several years after refeeding, because life and developmental stresses may precipitate a recurrence. Refeeding, re-education of eating habits, and explanation of physical symptoms are only initial goals in the treatment of anorexia nervosa, and continuing therapy has to be made available for many patients.

This means that the woman may need to know that she can contact her therapist at any time and to have regular appointments with her therapist over a number of years. In these sessions, the aim is to help the woman continue to escape from the preoccupation with weight gain and food that she had when she was ill, and to help her cope with life stress and other problems which may arise, without resorting to her previous disordered eating behaviour.

Death due to anorexia nervosa gets newspaper headlines, particularly if a celebrity such as Karen Carpenter is the victim. However, fewer than 5 per cent of patients die from the effects of the illness. In short-term studies, predominantly of adolescent women, the death rate is about 2 per cent. Long-term studies, which include the 20 per cent of chronic anorexia nervosa sufferers, suggest that 9 per cent of these patients will die over a period of years.

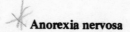

Anorexia nervosa

Summary of treatment of anorexia nervosa

* Age 18 or more
* Clinically not severely ill
* Failure of hospital treatment previously

* Age: less than 18
* Severely ill on clinical examination
* The woman expresses a preference

Usually treat as out-patient

*Offer suggestions and support
to help patient to:*

* increase weight slowly
* stop using weight-losing behaviour
* learn 'sensible' eating patterns

if not achieved

Usually admit to hospital
* Evaluate biochemical status
  *Provide programme to
  help patient to:*
* increase weight more rapidly
  1–2 lb (0.5 – 1.5 kg / week)
* cease weight-losing behaviour

Throughout programme provide :
* supportive psychotherapy
* help for other perceived problems
  (marital, family, medical)
* help in learning 'sensible' eating
  patterns appropriate to life-style

Later provide help for patient to :
* stabilize weight in desirable range
* continue to avoid dangerous
  weight-losing methods
* decrease preoccupation with
  weight and food

Overall aim is to help to:
* live a normal life
* be able to cope with life

8

Bulimia or binge-eating

I think that I look forward to a binge-eating session. Exactly what I am thinking is vague, but on reflection it is: 'Oh good, I won't have to think about dieting any more – what a relief'. If anything happens which delays the start of the binge I become quite angry and rather rude to the person who caused the delay. This anger is not warranted and is totally inappropriate – it could be likened to a temper tantrum.

Bulimia was considered to be a part of anorexia nervosa until recently, as it was observed that about 40 per cent of anorexia nervosa patients episodically lost control of their eating behaviour and binge ate. Bulimia is now accepted as a separate illness, but many of the features are similar in both illnesses, and some bulimic patients develop anorexia nervosa. The prevalence of bulimia in the community is unknown but the illness affects at least one woman in 50 aged between 15 and 35. The true prevalence may be higher as only those women who seek medical help are identifiable. Even these women may not be diagnosed as bulimic. Most do not tell their doctor about their eating habit, and as a result are investigated for gastrointestinal problems, such as a spastic colon, or gynaecological problems such as infertility and menstrual disturbances, or are thought to be depressed and are given antidepressants. In the past the majority of binge-eaters only received help because of an excessive weight gain (or a weight loss) or because of an attempt at suicide, but now, because of recent articles in women's magazines, many bulimia patients seek help earlier.

Binge-eating usually starts between the ages of 15 and 24 and follows a period of increased concern about body weight and appearance, during which the woman decides to diet or at least to 'watch' her weight. This is demonstrated by the fact that over 90 per cent of bulimia patients consider that they have been overeating before starting to binge-eat. Some have attempted to control their weight by sensible dieting which has been associated with a reasonable loss of weight for a

Bulimia or binge-eating

period of time. The desired weight loss of other women has not occurred satisfactorily in spite of fasting or adopting 'fad' or 'crazy' diets.

The woman develops an exaggerated concern about her body shape and weight, and this leads to more stringent periods of dieting, with episodes of binge-eating when the control over food intake weakens.

Case history: Jill

When I was 15, I looked at myself and thought: 'I'm too fat, and hate the size of my thighs and bottom.' My weight was then 9 st 12 lb (63 kg). So I started to diet taking in only 1200 kcals, and got my father to buy an exercise bike which I rode for an hour each day. I lost 11 lb (5 kg) of weight. In the next year I exercised a lot but ate normal meals and didn't gain weight. Then I got hepatitis and was in hospital for six weeks when my weight dropped to 8 st 7 lb (54 kg), but it built up to 8 st 13 lb (57 kg) in a few months — and that's the weight I think I look best at. So I was happy.

I went to 'Tech' when I was 18 and had a permanent boyfriend. We got on well but I started eating more and exercising less and my weight

Fig. 13. Bulimia.

81

went up to 9 st 6 lb (60 kg). He said I was getting fat and so did May, a girl in the class who was really fat. I don't know if it was what they said, but about then I began to be very aware of women's bodies, and how much they varied in shape. I began to be quite obsessed with body shape and how it was often out of proportion and ugly and I began to diet to get my body into a better shape. It didn't do much good because my body remained the same shape and I didn't lose any weight although I tried for a year. I think I became convinced that I couldn't eat as much as other people because if I did I would get really fat like May.

Then my boyfriend and I split up and I was sure it was because I was fat. I started taking slimming pills − I suppose I took more than 20 of them some days. They didn't work either, so I tried I don't remember how many diets. I tried staying awake all night because I'd read that mental activity helped lose weight. I went to a doctor who gave injections to dissolve fat, but that didn't work either. I tried wearing plastic to lose weight. I tried hypnotherapy. And once, when I had 'flu I stood under a cold shower and then went outside in winter for two hours to try and catch pneumonia. I even stopped taking vitamin tablets because I thought that there might be calories in the capsules. Nothing worked for me, and my weight stayed between 9 st 12 lb and 10 st 5 lb (63−66 kg). It was very discouraging.

I felt the only way that I could really lose weight would be to starve. And I did, but I got so hungry that when I had fasted for two or three weeks, only drinking fluids, I would binge-eat. I used to got out late at night and buy food or if I could, steal it. I tried to induce vomiting after the binge by sticking my fingers down my throat but I couldn't manage it so I started taking quantities of laxatives, and when, after a binge my ankles were swollen, I would get diuretic tablets from the doctor. My eating was really out of my control.

In fact I saw several doctors but none of them seemed to think there was anything wrong with me. So one day I took a large quantity of aspirin − I can't remember how many − to try to draw attention that I needed help − I really did need help!

Three years later she wrote to the clinic:

Looking back I think the reason I started binge eating was because of my obsession with dieting which stemmed from the fact I didn't realize in the first place that I wasn't overweight but that I had inherited fatter legs and thighs than the average person.

The onset of bulimia may also be associated with stressful life events, which are not related to the woman's concern about body image or weight. A domestic argument, illness or death in the immediate family,

the stress of examinations, a change in job, breakdown of a relationship, divorce, or pregnancy may precipitate the first eating binge. The
age of the woman has a bearing on which of the life events will precipitate binge-eating. Family problems or failure to achieve independence
from parents, are more common precipitants if the woman is teenaged,
while above the age of 20, marital and relationship difficulties are more
common. Some binge-eaters seem to have certain personality disorders,
others have a normal personality. It is unclear whether the personality
characteristics of binge-eaters have any relevance to their illness, as
they also occur among women who do not binge-eat.

THE EATING BINGE

*It is easy to convince yourself on the day after each binge that that was
the last one, and as of today you are never going to binge again. Unfortunately the nausea and feeling of self-revulsion disappears after a
few days and before you know it, the idea of escape into a session of
eating unlimited amounts of anything that takes your fancy gets hold
of you again. This can be caused by boredom, anxiety, or just a desire
to relax or escape for a while.*

Most binge-eaters are secretive about their behaviour. Many prepare
secretively for the binge or plan for it by hoarding food beforehand.
During the binge, as well as 'raiding the fridge', the woman usually
prepares simple meals for herself, but some women prepare and cook
elaborate dishes such as biscuits, cakes, and casseroles. Some women
buy food especially to eat during episodes of binge-eating. About half
eat most of their food during a binge in cafés or milk bars, or go from
shop to shop buying food and eating it immediately.

Most bulimia patients gulp their food quickly during an eating binge,
some stuffing food frantically into their mouth, often making a considerable mess, leaving empty open cans around. Other women are
careful to make no mess so that they may avoid being found out. The
rate of eating during an eating binge varies between individuals and
between binges. If the woman knows that she will not be disturbed,
she will eat more slowly, particularly if she knows she can induce
vomiting without being discovered. In general the rate at which she
eats becomes slower as the binge-eating episode proceeds.

Eating disorders – the facts

The binge may start at any time of the day and end as suddenly, but about one-third of binge eaters have specific times, such as weekends, when they begin to binge-eat.

The amount of food eaten during an eating-binge varies considerably, and ranges from 3 to 30 times the amount of food usually eaten in one day. The 'pickers' eat less than the 'stuffers', many stuffers eating over ten times the amount of food that they would eat each day when not bingeing. This can provide a large amount of energy, exceeding more than 20 000 kcal (83.7 MJ) during days of 'bad binge-eating'. Those who eat large quantities of food are more likely to reach higher body weights, to use slimming tablets and diuretics, to prepare food for a binge, to eat all the food that is available, to eat inappropriate foods, to have nocturnal binges, and to binge anywhere. The 'stuffers' are more likely to use and abuse alcohol or marijuana and may make an attempt at suicide following the episode of binge-eating.

Many binge-eaters claim they go on eating until they have eaten all the food available. But when this claim is analysed it is found that they are usually referring only to what they describe as 'binge' or 'bad' foods. They define these as foods they do not allow themselves to eat at other times, for example cakes and ice-cream, peanuts, or biscuits. Only a few actually eat everything in the cupboards and fridge. By the time that most bulimia patients seek treatment, they either induce vomiting, or take purgatives, or both. This behaviour may take place during the binge or immediately the binge ends.

The binge-eating episode ends for a variety of reasons. Some binge-eaters say simply that they 'ran out of steam'. Others stop because they feel discomfort being nauseated or full. Others because they can no longer continue to binge secretively.

After the binge, most binge-eaters promise themselves that they will keep to their strict diet or will fast and will not repeat the binge. A few fall asleep, but most take up their usual activities as if the binge had never happened.

Once binge-eating had been recognized by other people, most binge-eaters admit to it and some of them occasionally indulge in binge-eating in front of family members or close friends. A few binge-eaters use this in a manipulative way against parents or husband, implying: 'look what you have made me do'. Others go to great lengths to disguise their behaviour for long periods and all are more secretive about self-induced vomiting and other methods such as purgation, than about binge-eating itself. They are prepared to admit to binge-eating but they guard against others knowing that they induce vomiting or take large quantities of laxatives which they see as reprehensible behaviour, while the binge-eating itself is something they cannot resist.

It is difficult to be certain what binge-eaters mean by the length of an episode of binge-eating, as they describe episodes ranging from 15 minutes to three weeks in duration. Some women, especially those who have only recently developed abnormal eating patterns, see their binge-eating as occurring in separate episodes, up to six in one day. Others, often those with long histories of binge-eating, describe episodes lasting for 'days or weeks'. By this, they mean that the urge to binge-eat is continuous and is present when they go to sleep and on waking, although it is obvious that they do not binge continually.

The frequency with which bulimia victims indulge in binge-eating varies considerably. Episodes of binge-eating may occur two or three times a week, whilst some women only binge twice a month or even less often.

FOOD PREFERENCE IN BULIMIA

Each of the binge-eaters we have heard about or have studied include food in their binges which they do not allow themselves to eat at other times, calling them 'junk food', 'fattening food', or 'bad food'. Food eaten during a binge is sometimes selected because it is easy to 'stuff down' at the beginning of a binge, and easy to vomit up. Some of our binge-eaters said that their binges consisted mainly of soft, milky, or fluid foods, whereas others said they used such foods merely as a means to assist vomiting, and ate them towards the end of the binge.

The amount, type, and nutritional content of food eaten during a binge varies widely both within and between individuals. Contrary to most binge-eaters' impressions that the food eaten during binges is exceptionally high in carbohydrates, analysis of records of food actually consumed in a binge revealed that they were just as likely to contain excessive amounts of fat or protein. A few patients become vegetarian in order to control their weight and change from binges of food which are high in fat content to binges of fresh vegetables, on occasions, for example, eating 5–7 lb (2–3 kg) of raw carrots in a day. The amount, type, and nutritional content of food eaten during a binge may be entirely dependent on what is available in the home. Some women will eat anything that is available including tinned food, baby foods, frozen food, and scraps from rubbish bins.

PRECIPITANTS OF AN EATING BINGE

There seem to be a number of factors which may precipitate an eating binge in a susceptible person. Most women say that before starting a binge they are unduly tense. Three-quarters say that loneliness or boredom precipitated a binge or that constant thoughts of food and a craving to eat, which they were eventually unable to control, were factors. Although many women diet rigidly between binges, only one-third say that hunger precipitates the binge.

A scenario might be that as the women are constantly concerned about their body-image and keep to a diet to reduce their perceived ugly shape, an episode of loneliness, unhappiness, or boredom triggers thoughts of the pleasure of the taste of food, and this leads to an eating binge.

Binge-eaters are aware that obesity is inevitable if they continue to binge-eat and do not take measures to control their weight. Their fear of fatness is as great as their love of food. Faced with this dilemma, two strategies are available to them. The first is to reduce the amount of energy absorbed from the food they eat by inducing vomiting during and after binge-eating and between binges. The second method is to diet strictly between binges. Some women choose to vomit as a strategy, others choose to diet. In addition to these primary measures, many binge-eaters in both groups use other methods of weight control, most of which are potentially dangerous. Between 75 and 90 per cent of binge-eaters abuse laxatives during a binge, at the end of a binge or between binges. The reasons are twofold. First purgation clears out the mass of 'bad' binge-food and the patient believes that it will prevent the energy being absorbed and converted into fat. Secondly, the use of purgatives relieves the fullness of abdominal discomfort and bloating which occurs after binge-eating. The quantities of purgatives taken

Bulimia or binge-eating

Table 4. *Food eaten during a 'bad' binge lasting 8 hours (as reported by a patient)*

---

3 loaves, 5 lb potatoes (chips); 1 jar honey,
1 jar anchovies (on bread); 1 lb rolled oats;
2 lb flour (as pancakes); 1 lb macaroni;
2 instant puddings, 4 oz 'nonpareils', 2 lb sugar;
1 large pkt Rice Bubbles

1½ lb margarine, 1 pint oil (for cooking), 4 pints
milk powder, 1 tin condensed milk (in porridge
on bread or in drink); 4 lb ice-cream

1 lb sausages, or meat rissoles
1½ lb onions

12 eggs (in milk shake, scrambled eggs)

1 lb liquorice (liquorice allsorts), 2 family-size
blocks chocolate; 1 lb dried figs, 2 pkts sweets;
6 'health bars'; assorted cream cakes (up to 12)
eaten while shopping; 1 lb sultanas (on bread or
in porridge)

Any left-overs found in fridge
1 bottle orange cordial

This amount of food gives a total of:

Energy	226 070 KJ (54 000 Kcal)
Protein	1071 g
Fat	1964 g
Carbohydrate	14 834 g

---

varies from 10 to 30 tablets of a laxative taken daily to a 'handful' taken at intervals.

Case history: Karen

I find it easy to pinpoint the beginning of my illness. It began with an experience concerning one of my fifteenth birthday presents: a box of chocolates. I was at an age where pressures for social acceptance were, to me, immense, and pencil thinness, to me, was a prerequisite for social acceptance and self confidence. I ate some of my birthday chocolates and was offered a suggestion by my mother; 'If you don't want to get fat, stick your fingers down your throat'.

Maybe this statement has more relevance than I'd previously thought. Mum's simple statement triggered off every emotional fear within me: 'I'll be fat — socially unacceptable — ugly — have no self confidence — no self esteem. . .' The fears were inexpressibly greater than I can even imagine now. My future, with those chocolates in me, appeared what can be plain and simply described as 'black'. My mother's suggestion seemed the only exit from the 'black future' I had prescribed for myself.

Naively I took this exit, which turned out not to be an exit at all but an entrance into hell. If only I'd known!

To induce vomiting was a revolting experience to me, but the fear of the 'black future' provided no alternative at all. Physical weakness and psychological euphoria followed my regurgitation. No matter how painful, or revolting, I'd found the key to freedom from that dreaded 'black future'.

I left school on my fifteenth birthday and found an increase in life's pressures. Coping became difficult, but I still possessed my 'key' to confidence and acceptance. I made a habit of vomiting after every evening meal and as the months progressed, I gradually lost weight, believing that I was becoming more attractive all the while. The fact that my food output by means of regurgitation was almost equal to my food intake, allowed me to indulge for longer periods of time in my means of relief from life's pressures — eating — without gaining weight.

I became increasingly aware of my increasing ability to relieve life's pressure through the intake of food. Although the induction of vomiting continued to be traumatic, the relief beforehand, and the euphoria afterwards were, to me, of no comparison to it. The vomiting became more frequent as the food intake rose and I accompanied my physically strenuous job with all the exercise I could muster. Some nights I could not sleep due to the immense guilt of either not having done enough exercise, or having allowed too much food to digest.

By the age of about 16, I found myself unable to cope not only with problems, but with spare time. Anxiety seemed to rule my existence and I could not relax without food. If, even then, I was relaxing, I'm unsure.

I felt revolting fat and ugly when I could not see all of my ribs when I looked in the mirror. I took a large daily dose of epsom salts, along with what progressed to 13 laxative tablets daily.

Fortunately, my weight only regressed to just below 8 stone [50.8 kg] at its lowest. But it took its toll of my life. For breakfast I would eat

Bulimia or binge-eating

8–10 slices of toast plus cereal. Then I would do the dishes, eating everyone's scraps in an anxious, embarrassed, hidden hurry. I would then disappear inconspicuously to the toilet, and bring up my breakfast. My nose often bled, as did my stomach, and ten minutes later (to the dot) I would become very weak, dizzy, and pale.

I suffered malnutrition to the extent that my menstrual periods ceased for six or seven months. My god, I accepted such as being normal!!

During the following year, I began to realize that I was too thin so I fought my conscience and established my weight at about 9 stone (57 kg).

My eating, cunning and patient as it was, had increased during this time and I was spending about $10 [£7] per day on food outside the house. This was quite substantial to me, for I was earning only $80 [£56] per week. Fortunately I didn't have to pay board.

It was about this time that my boyfriend became too heavy to pursue his career as a jockey. I worried about his future, I worried about myself, I worried about everything and my only relief was food.

Being immature and mixed up, I acted strangely and desperately. My boyfriend had become part of a new group of friends who were heavily involved with drugs of every description – from heroin, to magic mushrooms, to petrol and glue sniffing. This was beyond my capacity to cope. My 'other half' was dying and I was dying with him.

I knew subconsciously that I couldn't go on with him, nor could I go on without him. Without directly breaking up our relationship I acted in a manner which drove him and me 'up the wall'. I was subconsciously hoping that he'd break off our relationship and therefore I'd have it easier. It didn't work that way. He clung on, as I did. My eating worsened, my mind and soul weakened. He got deeper into the drug scene, and I began to follow but, thank god, he loved me enough to keep me out of that 'black hole'. I suppose I'd have gotten in elsewhere if I'd really wanted to, but although I got drunk a couple of times and tried a few drugs, they did nothing for me. Food was my relief – my drug!

I isolated myself with food as often as possible. My crazy, desperate behaviour dared, and received, the punishment it deserved. And one desperate day when I'd driven my boy-friend so hard he hit me and threw me down in the middle of the road, (I was trying to stop him going to the pub), I returned to his house, alone, and desperate. There was no food in the house, I had no money, and I felt that I could take no more of the torture I felt the world was inflicting upon me. I took a loaded shotgun from the wall, and placed the end of the barrel in my mouth. I mustn't have wanted to die, because I received a sensation of strength which took away my need to pull the trigger. Although I didn't

89

want to die, the desperation remained. I screamed and bashed the wall and cried for what must have been about an hour. After this I felt terribly weak. I returned to work but wouldn't speak to my boss, nor later to my family. They had no idea — nor did I want them to. I'd constructed an impermeable barrier around myself. I couldn't cope outside of it.

The next day I penetrated my barrier and began to feel my way into the world again, like a child's first adventure into a garden. I felt I had a new lease of life, when crash, down fell my depression and desperation, taking on a new and tighter grip of me. I desperately ate my way through the day, resenting everyone and everything, playing sad music and feeling sorry for myself (although I didn't recognise self pity then), and topping off the mountain of hate I had constructed against the world; or was it myself? I rather believe the latter.

I tried to escape. I went to Scotland and ate my way through my short stay there. I returned home and couldn't cope with a single day. To my parent's horror and disappointment, I quickly packed and moved. The torture followed me, pouncing on me which ever way I turned. I spent my time obliviously eating my way through each day. Trying to live, but to no avail. At weekends I'd try to get home simply for the sake of the available food. I'd eat Mum out of house and home and the self-hate and guilt built up more and more due to my reasons for going home. It hurt me terribly when my mother confronted me with the fact that she was aware of my attraction to home. I loved my family dearly, but I then felt like a leech, so I went home as little as possible.

I spent my evenings at the local shops, with immense fear of being caught there, and with the guilt and anxiety continually mounting. To be so totally out of control in sobriety seemed so terribly degrading. I couldn't cope with this life, so after five and a half years of bingeing and vomiting, I told my sister what I was doing. She arranged for me to see a doctor, who laughed at me and said 'What do you want me to do about it? Sew your mouth up?' I was temporarily numbed by this experience. The guilt and embarrassment then came on hot and strong, and I broke down crying in front of him. He then decided that I was crazy so he referred me to a psychiatrist.

She made me feel more acceptable to myself. Nevertheless, my obsession with food continued to increase. I couldn't bear to live with myself, so my psychiatrist arranged for me to be admitted to hospital as I wasn't improving.

If ever I've believed in my own 'God', its now, for by what to me is a miracle, I've been identified as addict, and have progressed to 12 days in a row without overeating or vomiting. I hadn't succeeded through one single day in over a year before this, and how I'd tried!!

Bulimia or binge-eating

With the aid of the addiction program, and AA philosophies, I've learnt more about myself and how to cope with life in the past 12 days, than I have in the 20 years preceding. I'm gaining confidence, hope and see life as I've only dreamed of seeing it. I have a long way to go to recovery and I accept this. I've told the truth to my family and close friends, who have accepted it well. I'm truly getting there, and I won't give in for I've too much to lose. I've now had a taste of how enjoyable and exciting life can be; so hopefully, I will be able to stay in the life I love so much, and hopefully maintain self-control for the rest of my life over my eating and vomiting.

About 60 per cent of binge-eaters take commercial slimming 'pills', which contain some form of laxative, and a number take appetite suppressing medications which may have an addictive property.

About 40 per cent of binge-eaters take large quantities of diuretic tablets, as they believe that the tablets will enable them to lose weight. Some women are aware that only fluid is lost, others believe that diuretics in some way 'dissolve' fat. And 10 per cent of binge-eaters abuse alcohol or drugs.

HOW DO BINGE-EATERS TRY TO RESIST BINGEING?

Nearly every binge-eater has attempted, at times, to resist the urge to binge. The methods chosen to resist the urge to binge-eat vary considerably. Some women feel a reduced urge if they keep no food in the house, buying only what is needed each day; others avoid cooking or going into the kitchen. Still others spend a long time chewing a mouthful of food to prevent themselves stuffing more and more food into their mouths. Other women avoid eating with the family or going out to social gatherings where food is served. A few women take more positive action by locking themselves in the bathroom, driving into the country where no food is available, or keeping no money in their purse. Still others try to divert their thoughts from food, planning to be completely occupied at all times, by knitting obsessionally, telephoning friends, or going out to meet people. Some undertake work with long periods of overtime, in jobs where no food is available; others try to keep to strict diets, or eat only minute quantities of food at a time and avoid food shops. Other women use exercise as a way of avoiding binge-eating. They spend long hours at the gym, play squash, or tennis, or jog for many miles each day. One woman was so desperate she attempted to wire her jaws together by passing the wire through her gums by passing the wire through her gums after using a local anaesthetic ointment. Another cut the tips of her fingers so that they would be too sore to induce vomiting, hoping that this would stop her from starting on a binge.

Information about 'resistance behaviours' used by a binge-eater is often helpful in devising treatment.

THE PHYSICAL SYMPTOMS ASSOCIATED WITH BULIMIA

Most compulsive eaters describe a number of physical symptoms associated with the binge. In addition physical symptoms may follow induced vomiting or laxative abuse.

During an episode of binge-eating, most of the women feel 'bloated' or 'full' and some observe that their hands and feet swell. One-third are nauseated or complain of abdominal pain. By the end of the binge, over one-third complain of headache and half of the women complain of tiredness.

About six bulimia patients in every ten habitually induce vomiting. Initially vomiting is achieved by stuffing the fingers or a spoon into the throat, but later many women can induce vomiting by inducing a strong contraction of the diaphragm and abdominal muscles, to force the contents of the stomach into the oesophagus and then to vomit. In each episode of vomiting many women regurgitate one to ten times until they are certain all food has been brought up. Some women use 'markers', beginning a binge with food such as red apple skin, lettuce, or liquorice which they can recognize in the vomit. A number of patients also use 'washout techniques': they keep on drinking water and regurgitating until there is no residue of food in their stomach, a process which can last up to half an hour. In most cases the vomiting episodes last from 5 to 30 minutes, depending on ease of vomiting and quantity. The women tend to exaggerate the amount of vomit, describing the amounts regurgitated in terms of buckets full, icecream containers full, or saucepans full. To avoid detection they vomit into disposable containers or plastic bags. In one case the mother of the binge-eater habitually collected the vomited material and used it to fertilize the garden.

Bulimia or binge-eating

Over 75 per cent of women take laxatives to purge themselves either during or immediately after the binge. In some cases the quantity of laxatives taken is considerable, ranging from three times the recommended dose to 'handfuls'. Many of the women are aware that the diarrhoea following excessive laxative intake may lead to electrolyte disturbances, particularly potassium deficiency, and avoid them by eating potassium-rich foods such as oranges or tomatoes.

One half of bulimic patients take 'slimming tablets' or diuretics to lose weight, and these women may also abuse the diuretics with an inevitable electrolyte disturbance, particularly a potassium deficiency, unless they take measures to prevent this happening. As many of them are aware of the problems of potasssium deficiency, they take potassium supplements or drink orange juice which is rich in potassium. In some cases severe potassium deficiency occurs which requires treatment in hospital.

Many binge-eaters develop menstrual irregularities, although in contrast to women who have anorexia nervosa, their body weight is usually in the normal range for age and height or they are slightly overweight. Up to 60 per cent of women who binge-eat cease to menstruate, becoming amenorrhoeic for at least nine months, and about one half have irregular or infrequent menstrual periods. The reason for the menstrual irregularity is not understood.

THE PSYCHOLOGICAL EFFECTS OF BINGE-EATING

Before starting to binge-eat, most women feel tense and anxious, have palpitations, or begin sweating. During the binge, most binge-eaters feel a sense of freedom; the anxiety or worry they had been experiencing lifts and they no longer have anxious or negative thoughts. If the woman chooses to induce vomiting, she may associate her reduced tension with the act of vomiting. At the end of the binge, most binge-eaters feel less tense and anxious, but may not like themselves because of what they have done to their bodies. They may feel guilty about inducing vomiting and panic that the binge may induce a weight gain. This in turn may lead to further anxiety and tension, with the result that they may start binge-eating once again. A vicious circle is established (Fig. 14).

If a binge-eater is unable to relieve her anxiety and tension; for

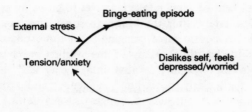

Fig. 14.

example if the person is interrupted or discovered when binge-eating, her behaviour may change to agitation, anger, or aggression.

It is also apparent that if a woman with bulimia does not recognize the tension and anxiety or has no other ways of coping with them, she easily enters the vicious circle and becomes a frequent binge-eater. As will be seen, a major objective of treatment is to break this vicious circle of eating behaviour.

Case history: Penny

I really started binge-eating when I was about 12. Before that I had bought lots of sweets, candies, and lollies, because Mum gave me a lot of pocket money — but all kids do that. Then when I was about 12 I started dieting and began binge-eating. I remember that I used to eat my pack lunch on the way to school and then scrounge food from the other kids. By the time I was 14 I was a real binge-eater. After a binge I would vomit and after a time I could vomit without putting my fingers down my throat. I still can, but I don't do it. What with study and fixing up bingeing, I didn't have time for friends. But it didn't seem to matter, I just had to binge-eat and I did, and then I vomited so that I wouldn't put on weight.

That went on until I was 20. I had this job — it was so boring and I hated it. One day after an eating binge, I was so agitated I drank half a bottle of sherry. It worked wonders. It steadied my nerves and I felt better. I started thinking that if I had a drink I wouldn't need to binge-eat. I bought a bottle of whisky and kept it in my wardrobe. When thoughts of food and putting on weight became overwhelming I'd drink some alcohol and they would be less insistent. That's how I stopped bingeing. I went on vomiting — it's easy to do when you know how and my weight dropped from 10 st 7 lb (67 kg) to 7 st 3 lb (46 kg). When I was drinking I was much more relaxed and began to go out with friends.

Bulimia or binge-eating

About this time I realized I was wasting my life so I left the dull job and stopped drinking except on social occasions when I would drink until I was drunk, or eat all the food I could. I guess the occasions gave me permission to indulge my needs. I started a secretarial course, which was hard work and one day I began binge-eating again. It was just after my 21st birthday when I had got drunk and had horrified my parents. Soon I was binge-eating three or more times a week. I started vomiting again and took large doses of laxatives. Because I was scared that I would put on weight even after what I was doing, I began to jog and was soon running 6 miles (10 km) a day. It seemed to help. When I was jogging I stopped thinking about food and weight, which stayed at 8 st 7 lb (54 kg) (100 per cent of Average Body Weight). Because of the vomiting my teeth were going bad, but I couldn't stop vomiting after an eating binge; it made me feel relaxed. And if I was having problems, or was worried I'd drop into the pub and have a few quick whiskys. Mind you, I was worried that I might be an alcoholic.

The next year I met Wayne and we married. It was great at first but I still needed to binge, and I did, often every day, and I kept a bottle or two of whisky hidden at home, just in case I needed a drink. When Wayne found out he was furious and I felt it was time I saw a doctor.

The Clinic records show that over the next three years, when Penny was attending regularly, she occasionally binge-ate, and twice returned to her previous behaviour of binge-eating three or more times a week and using alcohol. Her weight is stable at around 8 st 9 lb (55 kg), and she leads an active social life. Her employer says she is excellent at her job.

THE EFFECT OF BULIMIA ON BODY WEIGHT

Before developing the eating disorder the body weights of most binge-eaters are within the normal range. About 20 per cent are overweight or obese, and a similar proportion are underweight, often being diagnosed as having anorexia nervosa. After starting the binge-eating, many of the women show frequent swings in body weight. These facts indicate that women of all weights may binge-eat. Binge-eating occurs among obese women, women of normal body weight, and some anorexia nervosa patients binge-eat.

Case history: Jane

Jane started dieting at the age of 16 to control her weight. At first she had a small steady loss in weight. At the age of 17 she began binge-eating and for the next six years she alternated between binge-eating and strict, almost starvation diets, with resulting large swings of weight, of up to 3 stone (19 kg). When her weight was below 8 st 9 lb (55 kg), her menstral periods ceased, to return when her weight exceeded that weight. On two occasions of about two weeks' duration her weight fell below 80 per cent of Average Body Weight, placing her into the category of anorexia nervosa, as it is defined clinically.

Other binge-eaters control their weight fluctuations to within 6 lb (3 kg), by dieting and exercising excessively between binges, or by using vomiting and purging to prevent absorption of the food eaten during a binge. And, as has been mentioned, a number use intrinsically dangerous methods of weight control such as self-induced vomiting between binges or abusing laxatives, diuretics, and slimming-tablets.

THE TREATMENT OF BULIMIA

The one major element required for recovery from bulimia is a desperate will to live normally. Normality is the heaven for which I strive. Perhaps I will have it some day. I certainly haven't given up. This however is not as simple as it sounds to a binge-eater. It should be so easy to forget about counting calories and just eat three normal meals every day, but somehow the reassurance of knowing that you didn't eat more than your allowed calories is necessary. Without this reassurance, confusion can result, bringing on a binge. Counting calories doesn't mean dieting or denying yourself fattening foods — it simply means controlling your overall food intake and allowing for these fattening extras in your diet. It can stop the guilt associated with eating high-calorie items, a guilt which may be the cause of a binge.

The wide variation in eating behaviours of binge-eaters, the changes which occur in an individual over a period of time, the symptoms associated with binge-eating and the consequences which may arise, indicate that treatment has to be individualized and should be aimed to help the particular individual correct her disordered eating behaviour. Before treatment is offered the history of the illness and physical condition of the patient have to be assessed, so that her specific needs can be taken into account. Treatment may be geared mainly towards changing the patient's eating habits or mainly towards helping the person to cope with a specific problem. On some occasions family therapy may be required. In other cases relaxation therapy may be useful. If the person has a specific psychiatric problem not related to eating this has to be treated either before, or at the same time as treatment for bulimia. In such cases specific medications, particularly antidepressants, may be prescribed.

Four general statements can be made about treatment:

1. Admission to hospital and in-patient treatment is undesirable, unless the woman with bulimia has other psychological, psychiatric, or medical problems, such as depression, or is suicidal, or has a personality disorder which needs hospital therapy. The aim of in-patient treatment is to provide a supportive environment in which the woman can learn 'normal' eating habits and can cease to use the potentially dangerous methods of weight control, e.g. self-induced vomiting and purgative abuse. However, experience has shown that the improvement after hospital in-patient treatment is no better than that when the woman is treated as an out-patient. It also appears to have a potentially adverse effect on some patients: they take on the role of a psychiatric patient (as most admissions are to psychiatric units); they use manipulative behaviour, such as suicide threats, to gain repeated hospital admissions when facing personal, work, or other challenges; they use their 'illness' to avoid facing up to the usual problems that women of their particular age meet with; and they avoid responsibility for changing their own behaviour, expecting the hospital staff to take on this responsibility. Often within a few weeks of discharge from hospital the woman is binge-eating again.

2. If a stressful life event is expected, such as an examination, or the challenge of a new job, or if an interpersonal relationship ends, the woman must be warned that she may revert to binge-eating and the therapist should be available to talk with her and help her get through the crisis.

3. Binge-eaters should not take part-time jobs which are associated with food, such as waitressing, unless this is unavoidable, as association with food preparation or serving it is likely to provoke an episode of bulimia and to retard or to prevent recovery.

97

4. Until bulimia has been controlled for six months, holidays or trips overseas should be avoided. In an unfamiliar environment, with a loss of routine and frequent new experiences, it is common for binge-eaters to feel a loss of control of their eating and to revert to a pattern of binge-eating, self-induced vomiting, and purgation. A few bulimia patients resort to a starvation diet when on holiday because they fear that in the new environment they will lose control of their eating habits.

Binge-eaters can be extremely demanding of time, they can be manipulative and are not always truthful, as they are usually desperate for help and want the therapist to like them. Most realize that their behaviour is abnormal so it is not surprising that they are not always truthful. However, they have a great number of assets which makes working with them rewarding for the therapist. Even though not always appropriate, the resources they have developed, such as their resistance behaviour and their desire to get better mean that progress can be made, once the therapist has formed a good relationship with the woman.

The treatment of binge-eating, as with other eating disorders, is to alter the eating behaviour and to help the woman maintain her weight in the desirable range.

This is done by sessions of talking with a therapist during which the following matters are discussed and the woman learns:

- to acquire new attitudes to food and weight;
- to control her weight;
- to avoid inappropriate methods of losing weight;
- to recognize when she is in a 'bad mood'; and
  to learn to have insight into her mood changes,
- to recognize what precipitates binge-eating; and
- to find ways of coping with her problems, other than resorting to binge-eating.

Case history: Pat

I still have binges now – but they are shorter, they cause me less remorse and guilt and I consume less food during them than before. I simply can't fit the *volume* of food in I could before. I am fuller sooner.

Bulimia or binge-eating

They also relieve my anxious feelings better. I have the binge and I feel relieved. I can even sit and watch television for the rest of the night without continuing to eat because I am *satisfied*.

When I was caught up in it before, the night would dissolve into an endless foray in and out of the kitchen. I might stop for 1–2 hours (when absolutely full) but re-start eating later. Now, I usually stop and that's it — no more. (Although not always — I still experience a few binges like before and feel sick in bed afterwards.)

If I want to, I can stop the binge before it starts, or even *at* a point during it. But I have to say to myself: 'Why are you doing this? What's the matter? What are you trying to say to yourself?' or 'What are you unhappy about?'

Often the answer comes easily — 'I'm unhappy about Bill, I miss him' or 'I had a fight with Kevin and he boxed me into a corner again' or 'I'm hassled. There are too many things to do and I don't know if I can do them all in time' or 'My mother-in-law was here today and she annoys me. She seems to take over *our* house (even though I know she doesn't) and when she's here everything revolves around her' (she's a semi-invalid).

Sometimes I don't know why I'm bingeing (unlike before when I *never* knew why I was bingeing). And then I can't stop the binge.

Now the binges don't affect my weight that much. Firstly, they mean less food intake. Secondly, I can make up by eating sparingly the next day (and I usually am *not* hungry for a while). Thirdly, I can run or play squash to adjust my weight and enjoy the exercise.

How strange to feel 'satisfied' and happy with your life! It is the most superb feeling, to feel good about yourself!

I am pleased with my body and what it can do for me (in terms of sport or sex). It is not as skinny as I had wanted nor is it a model's figure. But it suits me and two men have lately confirmed that, saying things I would never have thought possible, like 'you have a little bottom' or 'I like your legs'.

I have treated myself to the luxury of new fashionable trendy clothes — a joy from the days when I dreaded trying on jeans because even size 14 never fitted me. In fact, many of the clothes from previous seasons look dowdy and very boring now — they represented a me who was afraid to show any of her body, who wore discreet plain clothes so as not to 'show off' and who never looked sexy because a fat person had no *right* to be sexual.

I know my body attracts men. I can feel the 'vibrations' or I can feel them watching me sometimes. This confirms my feelings of self-confidence in myself but also perhaps suggests that the new-found sexuality is showing. I feel a 'complete' person – all the pieces are there fitting together correctly – including the sexual part of me – and I guess it shows.

Binges for me are also a way to relax. I always keep little activities to do around the house so I am 'busy' and occupied away from food. But if I am tired or don't want to do them, then sometimes I'm stuck. I want to unwind and food is a good way. It involves little mental effort, it calms the nervous feeling in my stomach and it takes my mind away from work or troubles.

Changing attitudes to food and weight

In the back of my mind, I still feel that – should events one day go bad in my life – I could return to the bingeing as before. If there was too much pressure, worries or if I couldn't cope with problems, food is the crutch to keep me going. It would have to be very bad, but I also think I would seek help from my counsellors to keep me from turning entirely to food. I'm not sure – it exists as a possibility. Certainly, if I was bored, unhappy with my lifestyle (for example, stuck in a little house with a baby and no friends or money to buy things) or doing things I did not really want to do – food or eating might become the only interesting facet of life (as they were once to me). But I hope not. And I think – I really think – I'll make it without food in the long run.

Women who binge-eat, like patients with other eating disorders are pre-occupied with food and weight. They have to be encouraged to stop keeping food records, weighing themselves frequently, constantly counting calories, cooking for others, and reading recipes. However, it may be helpful at some stage in counselling if they mark the days of binge-eating on a calendar so that the frequency of bingeing can be discussed. The two findings which often arise from these records are that the incidence of episodes of binge-eating may decrease but not be recognized by the patient and that the frequency of binge-eating may be increased premenstrually and during early menstruation. Patients find it reassuring to know these facts.

Binge-eaters should be encouraged to eat out socially and increase other social activities. Most of them have withdrawn from social occasions because of the presence of food or because of feelings of social

100

unease, not related to food. They need help to find out what social eating is and to learn to incorporate it into their life-style. The fewer diet restrictions there are the easier this is. It also means giving up the distinction between 'good foods' and 'bad foods'.

Control of weight

As most bulimic patients have experienced large swings in body weight during the years of binge-eating, part of the treatment is to help the woman learn, often for the first time, how to stabilize her body weight and maintain it within the 'desirable' range. But first the woman and the therapist have to agree upon a sensible weight, which the patient will seek to maintain. This is usually only a problem with patients who have previously been at very low weights, as they may wish to remain or achieve low body weights which are difficult to maintain, unless the woman is preoccupied with food and dieting, which hinders progress to recovery. It is interesting that many patients who have been at high body weights often select as their desired weight one which is still above the normal range, for example, a Quetelet Index greater than 29, or greater than 120 per cent of the Average Body Weight. The woman must understand that she is not expected to keep her weight exactly constant, as fluctuations of 1 or 2 lb (0.5–1.0 kg) either way are normal, and should be expected. Unless the woman is aware of this, she may respond to an increase of 1 lb (0.5 kg) with panic, and this may precipitate an episode of binge-eating. On the other hand she may respond to a small loss of weight by thinking that she can eat more and this may start an episode of binge-eating. For these reasons a bulimia patient should avoid weighing herself more frequently than once a week, as this may precipitate feelings of panic, inadequacy, or failure.

A binge-eater has to learn to control her disordered eating behaviour before trying to reduce her weight, as any serious attempt at dieting will usually result in binge-eating episodes. This requires frequent discussions with her therapist, and often with a dietitian.

The object of these sessions is to help the woman learn to eat the appropriate amount of food required to maintain her weight. To help her resist binge-eating, the food should be divided so that she eats at least three times each day. To help her achieve this objective dietetic counselling may be helpful, as many patients no longer know how much they can eat in order to maintain weight. When patients describe the amount of food they feel they can eat, they do not take account of their binge-eating. For example, many patients are convinced that if they eat more than 1200 kilocalories (5.0 MJ) a day they will put on weight, and they claim that they have to keep themselves on a reducing diet when not binge-eating. It may take some time for patients to have enough confidence to accept that when they cease binge-eating, self-induced vomiting, and purgation they will be able to eat more at meals without weight gain.

Avoiding inappropriate weight-losing behaviour

Although many binge-eaters are aware that 'starvation diets', self-induced vomiting, and laxative and diuretic abuse are potentially dangerous, their knowledge is often inaccurate. Treatment of binge-eating includes discussion of the use the woman has made of weight-losing methods and her willingness to reduce their use. Many women who binge-eat are willing, at least initially, to try to change their behaviour, and are reassured when they learn about the effects which may occur. Most are unaware that they may gain weight temporarily when they cease the behaviour, as they retain fluid in their body. Most do not know that after ceasing to use the behaviour, constipation may persist for some time, as well as a feeling of abdominal fullness and cramps. As these women are preoccupied with body weight and abdominal fullness, such symptoms make them anxious, which may precipitate self-induced vomiting and purgation. It is often helpful for her to think of the symptoms as 'withdrawal symptoms' which she will have to suffer for a period of time. After ten days of no such behaviour, most patients usually feel comfortable; and after three weeks they usually report feeling better than they ever have, especially with respect to fatigue. Unfortunately it takes most patients some time to have the confidence to stop their behaviour completely, because they fear a rapid weight increase and loss of control of eating. It is difficult for them to be able to feel that their binge-eating will lessen if this behaviour stops.

Recognition of negative (dysphoric) moods

Patients describe anxiety, tension, and unpleasant moods prior to binge-eating. In most, the negative mood is relieved during or after the binge. Recognition by the patient of the association between unpleasant moods, especially anxiety, and relief from them by binge-eating assists her to find other more appropriate ways of coping with tension. Relaxation therapy can help, if only to enable patients to recognize their anxiety. Many patients find relaxation difficult at any time and almost impossible prior to a binge when they are most agitated and tense.

As the frequency of binge-eating decreases, the woman can discuss her need to eat in the face of stress. Once she understands herself a little better, she can reorganize her life-style to minimize eating due to stress, for example when examinations are approaching, by working more consistently without a last-minute cram; or by studying in a place which does not have easy access to food, by learning to have confidence to ask questions of, or help from, lecturers and tutors rather than worrying about what she does not know; or by arranging activities so she does not spend all day feeling she should study and eating as an excuse not to start.

The recognition of precipitants

The patient and therapist explore and discuss those factors, such as marital stress, loneliness, tenseness, and boredom, which have precipitated binge-eating in the past and currently. Recognition of precipitants to binge-eating assists patients to reorganize their life-style either to avoid these situations or to find other ways of coping at these times. It is interesting that as patients improve they recognize hunger as a precipitant but also explain that previously they had trouble recognizing accurate cues for hunger and satiation.

Encouragement of resistance behaviour

As was mentioned earlier, most binge-eaters have tried to resist binge-eating at some time or other. The methods they have used are many and various, and exploration of these with the therapist can give the patient insight into the problem. Some of the less extreme behaviour can be used successfully at times by patients and can be included in treatment programmes. Reorganization of life-style so that patients are occupied at the times they are most likely to binge-eat is useful, for example, attending a gym on the way home from work and before dinner, washing hair, and knitting when at home at night. Patients need a number of these interests, as they tend to become less effective over time, and the patient must enjoy the chosen occupation. For example if a patient hates jogging there is no point in doing it. Taking up interests also helps patients to feel better about themselves and feel more like other people.

Treatment of the physical symptoms

Most bulimia patients require little medical treatment for their physical symptoms. When treatment is needed it is usually because the woman has developed a potassium or a vitamin deficiency because of 'starvation diets', or self-induced vomiting, or abuse of slimming tablets, laxatives, or diuretics. In a few cases, treatment is needed because of a suicide attempt.

The symptoms of physical discomfort described by patients during or after binge-eating are: swelling of hands and feet, abdominal fullness, fatigue, headache, nausea, and abdominal pain. The swelling of hands and feet appears to be associated with the amount of food eaten and this symptom may be used by patients to obtain prescriptions from doctors for diuretics. The presence of the other symptoms appears to be associated more with the presence or absence of induced vomiting.

Many bulimia victims have disordered menstruation. Their menstrual periods either cease or occur only infrequently. In the past these young women have been subjected to endocrine investigations because of the menstrual disorder. Following the investigation they have been prescribed hormonal tablets to restore their menstrual function. The treatments have usually failed. Investigation and treatment of menstrual disturbances is rarely needed, as the menstrual pattern will return to normal once bulimia has been cured.

During the illness, the woman needs reassurance that she will not become sterile as a result of the menstrual disorder and she must use contraception if she is sexually active, as pregnancy may occur.

The menstrual disturbance may be associated with low body weight in a few patients but usually appears to be associated with the eating and weight-losing methods rather than low body weight.

Bulimia or binge-eating

Socio-medical problems

Many bulimic patients have problems relating to their age and their life-style which they have been unable to discuss with others. When they feel confident in their therapist they are able to start talking about these problems. In adolescent women a struggle may be going on between the woman and her parents, over her independence and the parents need for a dependent child. Other bulimia patients are ill at ease in social situations, have a low self-esteem, and are uncertain of the direction of their life. They may find it difficult to relate to others, which can cause friction in a marriage.

THE RESPONSE TO TREATMENT

The binges still occur but I would define them now as 'overeating'. My weight has gone up 7 lb (3 kg) but it doesn't bother me. I don't weigh myself anymore, at least not often. I don't try to stick to a diet as it would just emphasize food once again (but I'm sure that I will always count calories in my mind – but only in hundreds). I feel happy and try to eat normally whenever possible.

A good response to binge-eating is: (1) that the woman ceases to binge eat, or binge eats less than once a month; (2) that she ceases to use potentially dangerous methods of weight control, such as self-induced vomiting, purgative abuse, slimming tablet abuse, or diuretic abuse; (3) that she is able to stabilize her weight; (4) that she eats regular meals with no oscillation between overeating and starvation; (5) that she is able to interact with others of both sexes in social situations.

An intermediate response is that the patient shows; (1) a decreased frequency of binge-eating; (2) a decreased use of potentially dangerous methods of weight control; (3) stabilization of weight; (4) eats meals regularly; (5) develops improved social interactions; and (6) feels she has more control over her eating behaviour.

Case history: Yvonne

It's so good to feel 'normal' about eating and my weight now. I eat whatever I feel like, including cakes, an occasional chocolate, honey, bread, puddings, rich savoury dishes like quiche or pies. I eat when I want to, but I have found that I enjoy food most when I *am* hungry and can sit, eat leisurely and savour it. I have also found that my stomach will signal when it's full (although it's too easy to miss the signal at times) and I usually stop eating then. It's like regular people who eat when they're hungry and stop when they're full.

My appetite varies tremendously. Sometimes I will be hungry in the morning and eat breakfast, followed by something at 10.00 or 11.00 a.m., and then a bite at lunch. Other times, if I've had a big meal the previous night, a cup of tea takes me through till 12.00.

It amazes me how little food I need to satisfy my hunger at that moment. However, if I discover myself constantly in the kitchen searching for 'something' simply to put in my mouth, I realize I am bored or uptight and am seeking a pacifier. Then, I ask myself *'Exactly what* food appeals particularly?' Often the answer comes back 'Well, nothing really' or 'I don't know' and then (if I feel like it) I will say to myself 'You're not hungry really; you're just looking for a diversion' and go away to find something else to do.

My weight varies in cycles (this being deduced, not from the tyranny of the bathroom scales, but from the looseness of the clothes around my waist and bottom and the actual look of my stomach and lower chest — slight rolls being apparent at the heavier weight/

My weight does not worry me, nor do I try to control it by strict dieting. If I feel 'heavy', I will eat less food and drink, watch carefully for that point of stomach fullness and exercise more (running, dancing, gym classes, tennis).

There are cycles of heaviness when I feel heavy and have been over-eating and even non-aggressive binges. It's nice to know the connection between weight and eating. I know I am eating more and I feel my weight going up — not like before when I always seemed 'fat' regardless of how much or how little I ate.

Then there are slim cycles when I feel slimmer, trimmer and eat less (no sweets or dessert after dinner, no wine, no lunches out, no picking) but this just happens and I do not control it or feel guilty about eating less or more. . .

Recently, under much pressure of work and relationships, I started experiencing a 'knot' in my stomach, thinking it may be the start of an ulcer!

It immediately reminded me of my binge days when I often had this knot and thought it was stomach (i.e. physiological) hunger. Then, I would eat to relieve the 'hunger'. Food soothed away the pain and did, in fact, make me feel 'better', no longer being plagued by a gnawing in the stomach. However, when I ate food or drank milk to relieve the knot, it relieved it temporarily but then left me in 5 minutes again feeling the same. It was a tension build-up and I learnt I could relieve

Bulimia or binge-eating

it by deep breaths (trying to relax) or walking around and stretching. It went away after a couple of weeks.

About 40 per cent of binge-eaters, followed for a period of two years, show a good outcome to treatment, 40 per cent show an intermediate outcome, and 20 per cent show no improvement.

A good outcome is more likely if the woman is less than 20 years old when she seeks help and if she has been binge-eating for less than five years. In other words if the young woman, or her immediate family had a greater understanding of bulimia, she would seek help earlier and could expect a more rapid cure. The more difficult problem to overcome is the delay of binge-eaters in presenting for treatment. In part, this results from the patient's secrecy about her eating behaviour and in part from a lack of knowledge by doctors about binge-eating. Unless the woman is seen by the doctor after having made a suicide gesture, or is so emaciated that she appears to have anorexia nervosa, or is morbidly obese, bulimia is not considered a possibility by doctors. Many binge-eaters who go to their doctors are extensively investigated for their menstrual problems (often including gynaecological operations), or are diagnosed as having an 'irritable colon', or are prescribed antidepressants, which they usually do not take.

Relapses to binge-eating are not uncommon and are usually precipitated by a new life stress such as an impending examination, a change of job, illness, marriage, divorce, abortion, or the birth of a dead or deformed baby. It is of help to an ex-bulimia patient to know that she can seek help from a therapist whom she knows and with whom she feels comfortable should a relapse occur.

Bulimia patients should avoid becoming pregnant until they binge-eat less often than once a week. This advice is particularly important if they frequently abuse laxatives or diurectics, as during pregnancy these drugs should be taken sparingly or not at all.

Eating disorders — the facts

Summary of treatment of bulimia

Treat as out-patient

Help patient to :
* stop trying to lose weight
* stabilize weight in desirable range
* stop using weight-losing behaviour
* learn sensible eating patterns,
  appropriate to life-style
* eat food at least 3 times a day
* decrease preoccupation with weight and food

↓

Throughout programme provide :
* supportive psychotherapy
* help for other perceived problems

↓

Once binge-eating and weight-losing behaviours have ceased,
if the woman is still overweight and wishes to lose weight,
sensible dieting may be attempted

↓

Overall aim is to help patient to :
* live a normal life
* be able to cope with life

9

Obesity

My other good news is that my weight isn't such a worry any more. I am still overweight, but I certainly don't feel the grotesque elephant I used to feel. I'm 11 st 6 lb [72 kg] at the moment which is low for me, and I haven't put on any weight for about seven months. I'm not really dieting I guess. . . . just eating pretty sensibly and that seems to be enough to keep my weight stable. I know its a slow and black way to lose weight, but this way my eating doesn't dominate my thoughts so much. I really do hope to get down to about 10 st [63 kg] by Christmas and at that weight I'd like to think I'll be slim and satisfied with myself.

Obesity occurs when, over a period of time, the net energy intake exceeds the net energy expenditure. The term net energy intake is necessary because it has been observed that when a person increases the amount of energy ingested an increase in energy output occurs, and the excess energy available for storage in the body is less than 100 per cent of that ingested. The excess energy is stored in two main places in the body. The first place is obvious when you look at an obese person, that is the energy is stored in adipose tissue. Adipose tissue consists of about 80 per cent fat, 18 per cent water, and 2 per cent protein. Two pounds (1 kg) of adipose tissue has an energy content of about 31 MJ (7250 kcal). The second storage area for energy is called the 'glycogen-water pool'. Glycogen is a substance found in muscle, and each gramme of glycogen is bound to 3.5 g of water. The combination of glycogen and water makes the glycogen-water pool. The exact size of the glycogen-water pool is difficult to measure, but it is thought to weigh between 7½ lb (3.5 kg) in a non-obese person and up to 12 lb (5.5 kg) in an obese person. One kilogramme of the pool contains about 4.2 MJ (1000 kcal) of energy which is released (together with 7½ lb (3.5 kg) of water) when energy is required and none is provided by food or drink. Only when the glycogen-water pool is almost depleted of

Fig. 15. Obesity.

energy is adipose tissue burned up to release energy.

Obesity is defined in several ways, one being when the Quetelet Index is 30 or more (see p. 14). The level of 30 has been chosen because statistics from life assurance companies indicate that above that level a significant increase in morbidity and mortality occurs compared with lower Quetelet ratios. The level is rather higher than that derived from life insurance 'desirable' or 'ideal' weight-for-height tables. These tables were obtained after one particular company, the Metropolitan Life Insurance Company, had analysed the height and weight data of a large number of men and women and had found that 'desirable' or 'ideal' weights fell within a range for men and women. By desirable, they meant that people within this range of weight were at the lowest risk of developing an illness or dying prematurely. When the 'desirable' range is related to the Quetelet Index the boundaries of the range of 19 to 24.9 fit approximately. People whose weight range lies in the Quetelet Index range of 25 to 29.9 are overweight and have an increased risk but it is trivial, and for this reason the Quetelet Index range of 30 or more has been chosen to define obesity (Fig. 7, p. 15).

110

Obesity

Studies in several western countries show that about 10 per cent of children are overweight or obese. By adolescence the proportion has risen to between 13 and 23 per cent of all adolescents, especially females. Individuals who are obese in childhood or adolescence have an 80 per cent chance of becoming obese adults. In western countries the prevalence of obesity peaks between the ages of 50 and 60 in women and about a decade earlier in men. The second main group of obese people become obese in adolescence (usually by the age of 15) and continue to gain weight progressively over the years.

The increase in the prevalence of obesity with increasing age is in part due to the continuing ingestion of more energy than is expended, in part due to a reduction in the amount of energy the body needs for its basal functions as age advances, and in part due to a reduction in the amount of energy expended in exercise. How many people are obese is difficult to determine. A study in the USA conducted in the early 1970s, using skin-fold thickness at two body sites (mid-biceps and subscapular) as an index of obesity, found that 4.9 per cent of American men aged 20 to 70; and 7.2 per cent of American women aged 20 to 70 were 'severely obese'. Severe obesity was defined in the study as being 50 lb (23 kg) over the desirable weight for age and height in the case of men, and 66 lb (30 kg) above the desirable weight in the case of women. A total of 7 million Americans were considered to be severely obese. Severe obesity includes morbid obesity, but as the criteria for morbid obesity are more stringent, the increase in weight above the desirable weight being at least 99 lb (45 kg) the prevalence of morbid obesity in the community is lower. A rough estimate is that one person in every 2000 in Western developed nations is morbidly obese.

A reason that obesity is so common may be that in an affluent society with a variety of foods and drinks available, most people tend to eat more and thus take in more energy than they need. This extra energy is converted into fat. Among people whose weight is considered normal an average weight gain of 6½ lb (3 kg) occurs between the ages of 25 and 45. Of greater interest is that many people show unpredictable weight changes over periods of one to three years. These weight changes usually lie between 4½ and 15½ lb (2-7 kg) and rarely exceed 22 lb (10 kg). From this information it may be concluded that weight gain of more than 22 lb indicates an eating problem.

Eating disorders — the facts

Why do some people become fat in childhood or adolescence and gain weight faster than normal as they grow older, tending to become severely obese in middle age? It is easier to start answering this question by listing factors which are no longer thought to be important in the case of most obese people, although one or more may operate in individuals:

- there is no increased absorption of food from the gut of obese individuals;
- there is no increase in thyroid deficiency among obese people;
- obese people do not appear to have a greater 'addiction' for sweet foods containing more carbohydrate than thin people;
- the evidence that obese people choose a diet with a higher energy content than do thin people is not impressive. Further in an experiment when obese individuals were given two foods of similar appearance, one of which contained a high-energy content and the other a low-energy content, they were unable to detect any difference in the two foods;
- there is no conclusive evidence that obese people are less active than thin people.

When these hypotheses are excluded, the reasons why people become obese continue to be obscure. A genetic origin for some forms of obesity has been postulated but is probably of minor importance. The theory is based on the observation that in many instances obesity starts in childhood, increases progressively over the years, and tends to recur in families. This observation is reinforced by surveys which show that four out of five fat children become obese adults, and half of the obese people had an obese parent.

A possible genetic reason which may explain these observations is that people who are fat, or will become fat, are 'programmed' to use the energy they absorb from food for their needs more efficiently than thin people. This means that people who will become, or who are obese use less energy for any given activity, including their resting metabolism, than thin people and the excess of energy obtained from food intake is converted into fat and stored. It is important to note that for all but the most active people, sedentary activities (which includes the body's resting metabolism) account for most of the daily energy expenditure.

112

Obesity

It is possible that obese people are genetically programmed to be more efficient in handling this proportion of their energy expenditure, although they use the same proportion of energy for exercise as lean people.

However, the explanation for the recurrence of obesity in certain families may be behavioural rather than genetic: fat parents may have fat children because the family enjoys food and are big eaters, food and eating are perceived as socially pleasurable and desirable. This is in line with the observation that obese dog owners tend to have obese dogs.

Another theory is based on the observation that an obese person has a larger number of fat cells in his or her body than a thin person. Until recently it was believed that fat cells only multiplied in the body until puberty. After puberty, if a person absorbed more energy from food than was expended by metabolic processes or by exercise, the excess energy was converted into fat and was stored in the existing fat cells which increased in size. It is now known that when faced with the challenge of fat to be stored at any age, the fat cells first increase in size, and when a critical size is reached, divide to form new fat cells. Once formed the fat cells never disappear. If a person continually eats more energy than she uses up, in every period that weight is gained an irreversible increase in the number of fat cells occurs, which in turn are able to store more energy in the form of fat, and the person becomes increasingly obese. If the theory is true, obesity should be prevented from childhood by establishing sensible eating habits so that the person avoids becoming obese. Once a person has become obese, particularly if severely obese, it is difficult for her to lose weight because of the large number of 'hungry' fat cells which 'demand' to be filled. In some way, messages reach her brain stimulating her to eat more. However, if the person has avoided becoming fat or is only slightly obese, fewer fat cells will have been produced and weight reduction is easier. Unfortunately, these descriptive observations, if true, do not help to identify what messages, biochemical or electrical, induce the person to adopt a disturbed eating habit.

The reasons why people adopt disturbed eating habits have been discussed in Chapter 3. Most people who become fat in adolescence are female, and one reason why they become fat may be that they have failed to reduce their energy intake after their growth surge (and consequently their energy need) 'peaked' at about age 14. By continuing to eat the same quantity of food after this time their energy intake exceeds their energy output and the excess is converted to fat.

Another theory involves stress. It states that obese people eat more to compensate for a stressful life event. This is unlikely as many obese people have been obese in childhood, but most stressful events occur during adolescence, or later. However, the theory involves behaviour, and altered behaviour may be a factor in obesity. Habit and learned eating behaviour may be important in regulating food intake. If parents who enjoy eating habitually provide large meals, their children are likely to develop the habit of eating large meals and obesity may result, possibly because of the production of larger number of fat cells in their bodies, as mentioned earlier.

Yet another theory postulates that obese people are less easily satiated by food, they feel 'full' more slowly. Unfortunately what makes an individual feel full after eating a particular amount of food is unknown, so that the theory is of little practical value in altering the eating behaviour of fat people.

In summary, the reasons why fat people become and remain fat are poorly understood but they must ingest over the years more energy than they expend. For example, if a person ate 300 kcals (1.26 MJ) more energy each day than she expended; and if the net gain of this energy was 100 kcal (after allowing for the increased energy loss due to increased heat production) a net gain of 36 500 kcals (153.3 MJ) which is equal to 2 lb (4 kg) of fat, would occur each year. Recently there is increasing evidence, in man, that behavioural factors in eating control are important in the regulation of body weight.

OBESITY AS A HEALTH HAZARD

The fact that a proportion of the population is obese and a smaller proportion is morbidly obese would be of little consequence if obesity was harmless to health. Unfortunately it is not, as was shown recently by a study group of the British Medical Research Council who stated:

We are unanimous in our belief that obesity is a hazard to health and a detriment to well-being. It is common enough to constitute one of the most important medical and public health problems of our time, whether we judge importance by a shorter expectation of life, increased morbidity, or cost to the community in terms of both money and anxiety.

The effect of obesity on health has been investigated by many researchers, and is shown in Fig. 16.

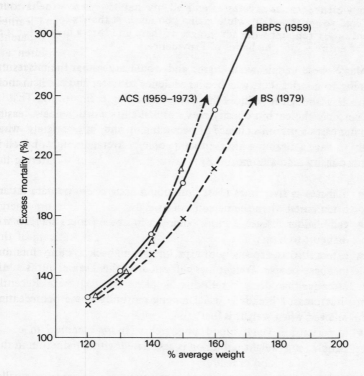

Fig. 16. Mortality increase with obesity. (The segments of the lines beyond 140 per cent of average weight in the case of the ACS study and beyond 160 per cent in the Build and Blood Pressure Study (BBPS) and the Build Study (BS) are extrapolations.)

It can be seen that a severely obese person has a three times greater chance of dying than a person of 'average' weight, and the more obese the person becomes, the greater is the mortality. Obese people tend to die young: obesity shortens a person's life.

In 1825 an obese man wrote a letter to his doctor:

Sir, I have followed your prescription as if my life depended upon it, and I have ascertained that during this month I have lost 3 pounds or a little more. But in order to reach this result I have been obliged to do such violence to all my tastes and all my habits — in a word I have suffered so much — that while giving you my best thanks for your kind directions, I renounce the advantages of them and throw myself for the future entirely into the hands of Providence.

Many obese people would agree and would argue that the misery of keeping to a strict diet, which does violence to tastes and habits, is not worth it, although it reduces the chance of dying prematurely. That is the person's choice; but obesity may not make life worth living. Obesity also increases a person's chance of becoming ill, and fat people are more likely to have a disabling disease than people of average weight. In other words obesity increases morbidity:

- diabetes is five times more common among obese people, and is often cured when the person loses weight;
- gall-bladder disease is more common in obese people and is more difficult to treat;
- osteoarthritis, especially of hips, knees, and back, is more common in obese people. Weight loss will not alter the disease, but is more effective than drugs in relieving the pain;
- shortness of breath is usual among morbidly obese people: it is relieved when weight is lost;
- hypertension (high blood pressure) is more common in obese people, and weight reduction is associated with a reduction in the level of the blood pressure;
- stroke is twice as common in obese people;
- coronary heart disease is more common in obese men, under the age of 40;
- menstrual irregularities (especially less frequent menstrual periods) increase as the weight increases, doubling in prevalence so that among severely obese women, one in four has irregular or heavy periods. Obese women are also more likely to be infertile than

women in the 'desirable' range of weight, mainly because frequently they fail to ovulate.

These rather negative findings may be converted to positive findings. If an obese person loses weight so that the weight lies within the desirable range for age, sex, and height, or the Quetelet Index is in the range 20–29, the person has less chance of developing diabetes, hypertension, a stroke, gall-bladder disease, and coronary heart disease than an obese person. And, as well, if the person has osteoarthritis it is likely to be less incapacitating. When an obese woman loses weight her menstrual periods become regular and, if infertile, she is more likely to become pregnant.

THE INVESTIGATION OF OBESITY

The physical examination

Three forms of investigation are required to be made before an obese person is offered treatment. The methods are (1) physical; (2) biochemical; and (3) psychological. These investigations start before treatment and continue while the patient is receiving treatment.

Table 5. *The advantages of weight reduction*

(1)	Reduction in blood pressure (both systolic and diastolic) (and consequently fewer strokes)
(2)	Improved cardiac function
(3)	Improved pulmonary ventilation
(4)	Reduction in pain from osteoarthritis and low-back pain
(5)	Improved circulation in legs with decrease in venous thrombosis
(6)	Reduction in fatigue : increase in energy
(7)	Increased self-esteem, increased social gregariousness, better 'body-image'
(8)	Increased physical activity can be undertaken
(9)	Improved sexual relationships

A full medical history and physical examination is made. The medical history includes questions about alcohol, smoking, and drugs. In women a menstrual and a sexual history is taken. The physical examination is that normally made for an insurance examination, including an estimation of the resting blood pressure, and an examination of the urine. The opportunity should be taken to evaluate those conditions aggravated by obesity such as osteoarthritis and high blood pressure.

Laboratory tests have a limited place in the general physical examination according to British doctors, although American bariatric physicians disagree. Dr Garrow, in Britain, states that most of the tests often carried out, for example, X-rays of the skull (pituitary fossa), plasma insulin levels; glucose tolerance tests, secretion of cortisol and catecholamines, are of little value in evaluating obesity. On the other hand, Dr Bray in the United States analyses blood samples for glucose, blood urea nitrogen, uric acid, alkaline phosphatase, total protein, serum glutamic oxalo-acetic transaminase, lactate dehydrogenase, bilirubin, thyroxine, triglyceride, and cholesterol.

Following the history and general physical examination, several specific investigations may be required to determine the most appropriate treatment and the probable duration of time required for the person to achieve his desired weight, particularly if the person is severely or morbidly obese.

Body composition

Most morbidly obese people have a large amount of adipose tissue, and their excess weight is mainly due to fat, but a few retain a large amount of water, which forms a significant component of their excess weight. It is important to differentiate the two types of people by determining their body composition. This can be done clinically and by using laboratory techniques. Both are required to fully establish body composition.

Clinical

The proportion of fat in the body can be inferred by making measurements of the thickness of a fold of skin at four sites on the body.

The following skin-fold thicknesses are measured by picking up a fold of skin and measuring its width with calipers (Fig. 17).

(1) *biceps skin-fold* over the front of upper arm midway between elbow and shoulder;

(2) *triceps skin-fold* over the back of upper arm midway between elbow and shoulder;

(3) *subscapular skin-fold* under the lower tip of the shoulder blade;

(4) *suprailiac skinfold* above the crest of hip bone.

The information obtained from the sum of the four skin-fold measurements is used to estimate the fat as a percentage of the body weight by referring to special tables constructed for each sex and age range. The results, when compared with the specific laboratory tests outlined in the next section, show that skin-fold measurement gives a close indication of the percentage of fat in the body.

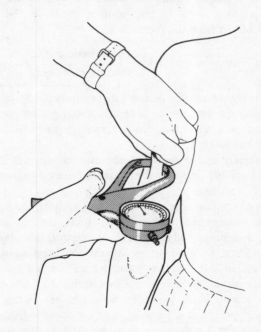

Fig. 17. Measuring skin-fold thickness with calipers.

Eating disorders – the facts

Laboratory tests

In research, two laboratory investigations provide a very accurate assessment of the body composition. These are discussed here to complete the picture, although it is realized that in clinical practice they are not usually available and the time and expense required to make them may not be warranted.

The tests are (1) to measure the total body potassium and (2) to measure the total body water. Both measurements are made with a mass spectrometer, which detects isotope release. The measurement of the total body potassium depends on the observation that all potassium (including that in the body) emits gamma rays. It has also been shown that the fat-free tissues of a man's body contain 30 mmol of potassium (K) per pound (66 mmol per kg) weight, and that of a woman 27 mmol K per pound (60 mmol per kg). By measuring the gamma rays released from the potassium in the body, the total body fat can be calculated from the formula:

$$\text{Fat content} = \text{Body weight in kg} - \frac{\text{total body potassium}}{66 \text{ (in men) or } 60 \text{ (in women)}}$$

The total body water of a person can be measured by giving a small dose of radioisotope deuterium oxide into a vein and by measuring the amount in the person's urine, blood serum, or saliva about 8 hours later in a mass spectrometer.

These two tests enable research scientists to estimate the Resting Metabolic Rate of the person – that is the amount of energy used for the basal body functions.

Individuals of the same sex, age, body composition, and body weight have different energy requirements for their resting, unconscious functions of breathing, body repair, heat control, intestinal activity, etc., and in addition, they use energy with different degrees of efficiency for muscular activity. In practice, muscular activity is a less important factor than the resting metabolic rate in determining a person's energy expenditure. Obese people generally have a higher resting metabolic rate than lean people, but the energy used by obese individuals differs considerably. This will influence rate of weight loss if an obese person chooses to diet.

Obesity

The resting metabolic rate (RMR) can be calculated from the formula:

$$RMR = 99.8 \text{ (Body weight in kg} \times 1.155) + \text{(Total body potassium} \times 0.0223) - \text{(Age} \times 0.456)$$

[handwritten margin note: the higher the rate is the easier to diet]

The result is expressed as the oxygen uptake in ml/minute. If this figure is multiplied by 7, a rough approximation of the resting energy expenditure is obtained.

For example, a person whose resting metabolic rate is 200 ml oxygen/minute uses about 1400 kcals (5.88 MJ) a day for the basic resting functions of his body; while a person whose resting metabolic rate is 270 ml oxygen/min uses about 1890 kcals (7.94 MJ) a day. If these two people are given an identical diet providing 1000 kcals (4.2 MJ) a day, the first will have a deficit of 400 kcals (1.68 MJ) a day, the second a deficit of 890 kcals (3.80 MJ) a day. Clearly the former will take twice as long to lose the desired amount of weight as the latter, assuming each takes the same amount of exercise.

THE MANAGEMENT OF OBESITY

As in the case of other eating disorders, the essential features in the management of obesity are first to help the person to resist the urge to eat and secondly to provide an easily understood, appropriately designed diet, which reduces the amount of energy taken in to a level substantially less than that expended. Treatment seeks to enhance the person's motivation to resist the urge to eat and to enable her to keep to her diet. If this fails, although the patient may lose weight in the first months of treatment, the weight loss will not continue and weight gain is inevitable.

Weight loss is a slow process, and the patient may become despondent about achieving it. The support, information, and encouragement offered by a group such as Weight Watchers or TOPS, or a psychologist or a physician will enhance the patient's motivation, encourage her skills, and offer help in dealing with situations which may trigger the urge to eat excessively. It is also evident that the greater the patient's original weight the longer will be the period required to enhance her motivation, and the greater the chance that she will abandon her attempts. In this situation, surgical intervention, in spite of its dangers,

121

may be appropriate, provided that the patient fully understands the implications of surgery and that the long-term 'success' rate has not been clearly defined.

Before the patient embarks on a weight reduction programme it is important for a physician to make sure that the weight loss is medically desirable and psychologically wise. It is even more important for the obese person to accept that an average loss of weight of 1-2 lb (0.5-1.0 kg) is the maximum usually obtained after the first few weeks (when a weight loss of 4-8 lb (2-4 kg) a week may occur) and the most appropriate diets are designed to help the person achieve this small but steady loss of weight. But, as in the treatment of anorexia nervosa or bulimia, a diet alone is not enough, motivation to resist the urge to eat and to keep to the diet is essential.

It will be recalled that excess energy is stored in the body in adipose tissue and in the glycogen–water pool. If a person starves in order to lose weight, or at least considerably reduces her energy intake, she extracts energy from the stores in her body to meet the energy needs. The first source of energy comes from the glycogen–water pool. The size of the pool varies. In non-obese people it weighs about 7½ lb (3.5 kg). In obese people it weighs about 12 lb (5.5 kg). It contains about 4 MJ (1000 kcal) per kilogramme. When energy is released from the stores in the glycogen of the pool, water is also released. For every 1000 kcal of energy released, 6½-8½ lb (3-4 kg) of water will be lost to the body in breathing, as sweat, or in urine. In the first weeks of a severe reducing diet, or of starvation, a quick weight loss may be expected as the energy in the glycogen–water pool is used up and a large quantity of water is lost to the body. However, the energy in the pool will be depleted within 1 to 4 weeks (when a weight loss of 6½-13 lb (3-6 kg) will have occurred). After this time, any further weight loss has to come from 'burning-up' the adipose tissue to release energy. The second component of weight loss is a slow, steady loss. The amount lost weekly will depend on the restriction of the energy intake, but rarely exceeds 1-3 lb (0.5-1.5 kg) per week.

An obese person who wishes to achieve a weight reduction of 7 st (45 kg) has to lose the equivalent of 1320 MJ (315000 kcals) as each kilogramme of adipose tissue contains 29.3 MJ (7000 kcals). If she takes a diet supplying about 4.62 MJ (1100 kcals) a day, which provides an energy deficit of about 4.62 MJ (1100 kcals) loss of weight over her energy needs each day, she should achieve this in about 10 months, but the rate of weight loss will depend on her lean body mass and on her metabolic rate. The higher her metabolic rate, the quicker will her weight loss occur, so that the time taken varies and only a range of time can be given to the individual, unless research laboratory facilities are available to calculate her resting metabolic rate.

Case history: Marjorie

It all started about 10 years ago, on my parents' 25th wedding anniversary, when my sister's husband deserted her. We were all living at home and we had endless family discussions, which became very emotional. And at the same time I became increasingly worried about the business ethics of my employers; they were crooked. These two things made me tense and angry all the time. To top it off my boyfriend had a bad accident and became very depressed so he needed my support. I felt that I was everybody's prop and couldn't escape.

I wasn't aware of it at first that my weight began to rise, until I found I needed a size 16 dress instead of a size 12. I tried to diet but the problems remained and food seemed to be the only way I could dull the pain. I got into the habit of looking in the mirror, being depressed at what I saw and eating some more so that I could cope. I dieted, and began losing weight and then I'd give it up and eat enormous amounts and gain weight once more.

My behaviour became destructive to me. I now knew I was using food as an escape from emotional pain and stress. I was really no different from an alcoholic, and I realized I wasn't going to conquer it alone but there was nowhere to go. I was on a roller coaster of eating and dieting and I couldn't get off. I didn't induce vomiting or take laxatives or anything like that. It wasn't as if I had thought of these things and rejected them — I hadn't even thought of them.

I knew I had an eating disorder. I wasn't in control, food was controlling me. I was a fat girl and I wanted to be thin, but I couldn't keep to a diet to become thin. I'm still a fat girl. I now weigh 13 st 7 lb (86 kg). I wish I could get thinner.

Diets

Several diets containing 4.6 MJ (1100 kcals) and providing adequate amounts of nutrients, minerals, and vitamins are available. Many diets are monotonous, and are likely to be abandoned, or are too complex to follow for a long period. If the person is to keep to a diet for 10 to 15

Table 6. *The principles of low-energy diets*

1.	It must supply *less* than the person's energy requirements.
2.	It must provide all nutrient requirements except energy.
3.	It must be acceptable to the person.
4.	It must be sustained.
5.	It must not impair health or well-being (e.g. low fibre diets may cause constipation).
6.	Its effectiveness will depend on the foods the person *refrains* from eating.

months, it must be reasonably easy to follow and should not distort the person's food habits or 'social' eating too markedly. In other words, the diet must conform to certain principles (Table 6).

Unfortunately, most obese people are unable to keep to the strict 4.20–5.0 MJ (1000–1200 kcal) diet for the period of time necessary to lose a significant amount of weight. Experience has shown that the weight loss in the first four weeks is crucial. At the end of this period of time, three outcomes are possible. First, if the patient returns having lost 8½–17 lb (4–8 kg) and says it was not difficult to keep to the diet, progress is likely to be satisfactory. Secondly, if the patient returns after, say, four weeks, having lost less than 6½ lb (3 kg) and says that it has been increasingly difficult to keep to the diet, or states that she has kept rigidly to the diet and has not lost a significant amount of weight, it is necessary to investigate the reasons for the poor weight loss. The most likely cause is that the person's home or work place environment is such that the temptation to overeat cannot be resisted. In this case additional supportive psychotherapy may enable the patient to resist temptation, or strategies can be devised to alter the situation in the home or work place. Thirdly, the person may return having failed to lose significant weight in spite of keeping strictly to the diet. These people require further investigations and possibly the measurement of their resting metabolic rate to determine the reason for the failure to lose weight.

The range of diets is wide, and the person can be offered a choice in the discussions which should take place before she embarks on a diet.

Obesity

Of the several choices available, two rather different diets have been recommended by doctors interested in treating obesity. The first which is used in Britain, is *the Milk Diet*. The second, which is used, sometimes in a modified form, by several specialists is *the Reduced Carbohydrate, Fat, Calorie Diet*.

The Milk Diet

The need to make decisions and the need to be motivated to keep to the chosen diet has induced some physicians to offer a diet which is easy to follow although extremely monotonous. The Milk Diet has been used in Britain with some success. It consists of 1800 ml (3 pints) of whole cows' milk, with supplementary iron and vitamins and, when necessary, an inert bulk laxative. The diet provides 4.9 MJ (1170 kcals) of energy and 59 g of protein. Those who use it claim that the Milk Diet has several advantages over other diets. These are (1) it is cheap; (2) no weighing of foods or need to make food choices is necessary; (3) the diet is not complicated or troublesome to prepare. The obvious disadvantage of the milk diet is its monotony and that it inhibits the patient's social life, as she is often unwilling to go to social functions where a variety of food is available. A more important criticism is that the Milk Diet does not help to alter the eating behaviour of obese people. The diet can only be used for a short period of time for the reasons given. When the person returns to a more varied diet, she has not learned new eating habits and may rapidly revert to the previous patterns.

In spite of these constraints, the Milk Diet may be of value to some obese people, at least during the initial weeks of dieting. Once some weight loss has been achieved, the person may transfer to a more varied diet which reduces the intake of calories, carbohydrate, and fat.

The Reduced Carbohydrate, Fat, Calorie Diet

An appropriate diet for weight reduction has first, to be effective in removing excess fat; secondly, to be palatable; thirdly, to distort the person's eating habits as little as possible; and fourthly, to become a permanent eating habit. It is for these reasons that the 'fad' diets and the crazy diets, which appear in magazine and book form at frequent intervals are rarely effective over a long period of time.

Eating disorders — the facts

Diets can be devised which meet the four aims, and one such diet is the *Reduced Carbohydrate, Fat, Calorie Diet.* The diet is designed to reduce the quantity of carbohydrate in the diet, by eliminating many sweet foods such as sugar, cakes, jams, and so on, while providing sufficient 'complex' carbohydrate, vitamins and minerals to avoid metabolic disturbance. The diet also reduces, indirectly, the amount of fat eaten, while retaining a normal amount of protein and fibre. The person choosing the diet has to make choices, but these are relatively easy to understand and to follow. The principal choice is to avoid eating 'prohibited' foods. In most cases the diet should be prepared by and discussed with a dietitian who evaluates the person's food likes and dislikes and formulates the diet taking these into consideration.

The main feature of the diet is that it is reduced in carbohydrate and most of the carbohydrate chosen is complex, such as is found in natural not refined foods. This means that you have to discipline yourself to cut down, or to cut out, some of the foods to which you have become addicted over the years. The first is sugar. Sugar is pure 'refined' carbohydrate and contains nothing but energy. That is why it is said to contain 'empty calories', for it provides no nutrients to the body. Sugar just provides energy, but in our Western diet the energy needed is provided as easily and more nutritiously in other foods. This means you must not eat honey, sugar, or sugar-rich foods such as sweets, chocolates, cakes, and ice-cream!

In any addiction, withdrawal of your 'drug' may cause upsets. When you stop using sugar you may find that you crave to add it to your tea or coffee or to your breakfast cereal. You can deal with this craving for sugar in one of two ways. Which you choose will depend on your personality. The first way is to stop at once. You stop using sugar in tea or coffee, you avoid using sugar on breakfast foods, and you stop eating sweets, cakes, or chocolates. The second way is to be more gentle to yourself. If you habitually add three spoons of sugar in your cup of tea, cut it down to two, and then after a few days to one. In other words, wean yourself gradually from your craving for sugar and sweet foods.

You must also restrict your intake of alcohol. Although alcohol is not strictly a carbohydrate it provides energy in the same way. And many of us enjoy a drink! Again, you can be very firm with yourself

126

and drink soda water with a slice of lemon and, if you wish, a dash of angostura bitters in place of your favourite drink. Or, if you are less strong, you can if you wish have half a pint (250 ml) of beer, or a nip (30 ml) whisky, or a glass (125 ml) of a light wine a day. Each of these provides a little under an ounce (25 g) equivalent of carbohydrate, or about 100 calories of energy. But you must not add bitter lemon or ginger ale to your whisky, or drink either of these alone, as they obtain a fair amount of sugar, whatever their taste. You can only have water or soda water which contains no calories.

The second feature of the diet is that you should avoid eating excess fats. You can do this quite easily by buying lean meat and cutting off the extra fat from other meat. As well, you should grill the meat rather than frying it. You may eat butter or margarine — but spread it thinly.

The third feature is that you should increase the food (or dietary) fibre content of your diet. Dietary fibre is that part of the plant (usually the husk or wall) which man is unable to digest. Increased dietary fibre is important for several reasons. First, if your food is rich in fibre you have to chew it more before you swallow it — and that means you tend to eat less. Secondly, increased fibre in your diet may reduce the amount of energy you absorb from your food. Thirdly, over the years, increased dietary fibre may prevent you from developing certain diseases of civilization, such as haemorrhoids, irritable bowel, diverticular disease of the bowel, and possibly cancer of the colon. You can obtain increased dietary fibre if you eat wholemeal bread or high-fibre white bread in place of ordinary white bread, potato in its jacket in place of peeled potato, and green leafy vegetables, especially spinach. If you eat breakfast cereal, choose a high-fibre muesli or make your own, and don't add sugar to your cereal.

As long as you accept these reservations you can work out your own diet, or seek the help of a dietitian. If you choose to do it yourself you may use carbohydrate units (one unit equals 5 g of carbohydrate) as suggested by Professor Yudkin who first thought of this type of diet, or you can calculate your carbohydrate intake in grams from easily available tables. If you choose to use grams you should restrict your intake to between 50 and 100 g a day, depending on how much you are overweight, how quickly you want to get rid of the extra fat, and how strong your will-power is.

127

Eating disorders — the facts

Since you only have to calculate your carbohydrate intake you only have to eliminate foods which contain significant amounts of carbohydrate. You can eat as much as you wish within the restrictions discussed of the following: meat, fish, eggs, cheese, butter (or margarine), green leafy vegetables, and most fruits. But you should not eat more than two or three slices of bread each day, and you should not eat cakes or pastries at all.

The attraction of this diet is that within certain limits you eat as much the same foods as the rest of your family, and so you don't feel outcast or different.

It may well be that while you are on a diet you are invited out to a dinner party. You don't have to be embarrassed, or embarrass your hostess, by toying with your food and leaving most of it on the plate. You just have to be sensible and enjoy yourself. You miss out the bread roll and the pudding unless it is a fresh fruit salad, and you limit the amount of alcohol you drink. You only take one potato, but you eat everything else. If you do exceed your daily quota of carbohydrates, well, it is a special occasion and it won't make much difference in the long run.

The suggested diet, which is low in calories and in carbohydrate and rich in fibre, has many advantages. It is nutritious; it is relatively easy to understand and to follow; it doesn't make you feel a freak; it avoids gimmicks; you can stay on it for a long time, and most important of all, it works! These criteria form the basis of a sensible diet for a sensible person.

But a diet will only work if you really want to lose weight and are prepared to understand and stick to the diet over a period of months.

In the end it is up to you, but you may need additional help to change your eating behaviour.

The behavioural aspects of weight reduction

A diet, in itself, will not enable a person to lose weight, however carefully it is devised and however many dietary cookbooks are made available. The person has to be motivated to keep to the diet and to understand it. Unless the person is motivated, she will find it easy to cheat — just a little! But lots of 'just a littles' equal a considerable amount of excess energy ingested. Motivation can be encouraged in

128

Table 7. *The Yudkin diet modified and simplified*

You can eat as much of these foods as you like — but be sensible!

Meat (lean)	Butter
Fish	Cheese
Eggs	Green leafy vegetables

You can eat a limited amount of these foods:

Milk (preferably skimmed)	Up to 600 ml (1 pint) a day
Fresh fruit:	Not more than two of the following a day: apples, oranges, grapefruit, pears, peaches; or one of the above and an average serving (about 4 oz (120 g) of strawberries, raspberries, gooseberries, plums, blackberries, cherries, or grapes

You must restrict these foods because they contain carbohydrate, although you can substitute one for the other:

Bread (preferably wholemeal)	Potato, average size
Oatmeal	Baked beans (which are rich
Biscuits	in fibre)
Cornflakes	Nuts

In a day you can have up to three slices of bread (depending on how quickly you want to lose weight) or the equivalent. Remember the calories content of the following is about equal: 1½ slices of bread = 1 average potato = 3 small sweet biscuits = 1 average serving of oatmeal porridge, or cornflakes, or baked beans

You must avoid these foods, as they are either completely or mostly carbohydrate:

Sugar (raw or refined)	Cakes and buns
Sweets and chocolates	Canned fruits
Jams and honey	Soft drinks (except
Pastries and puddings	soda water)

You should avoid alcoholic drinks, but if you can't, limit yourself to one of the following:

Beer	250 ml (½ pint)
Whisky	30 ml (1 measure)
Wine	125 ml (1 glass)

---

several ways, and the dieter requires to choose the way which she finds more appropriate for her.

Many people find that their motivation to lose weight is increased if the person can share her experiences with, and obtain support from, other people who are also trying to lose weight. The support needs to extend over a period of weeks or months during the period of weight reduction. Support is also needed when the person has achieved the lower weight, so that she does not regain weight swiftly or insidiously. Many obese women find it helpful if they join an organization such as WWI (Weight Watchers International) or TOPS (Take Off Pounds Sensibly).

Membership of the organization provides a stimulus to achieve a weight loss (by a system of rewards and demerits) and provides a form of group therapy. The value of such organizations is shown by a study made in Australia in which the weight loss of women attending a hospital-based obesity clinic was compared with that of women who joined WWI. The women who had joined WWI lost more weight each week and remained at the lower weight for longer than those woman who attended the obesity clinic.

Motivation and knowledge is also required because there is no magical, easy method of losing weight. It is fairly easy to lose 6½-13 lb (3-6 kg) of weight quickly, but it is difficult to prevent the relentless return of that weight unless the person is sufficiently motivated to continue eating fewer calories than are used up in daily living. Weight reduction is a slow process, but if a person is sufficiently motivated to keep to a diet providing 2.1 to 4.2 MJ (500 to 1000 kcals) less than is needed each day, stored fat will be burned up at a rate of about 1-2 lb (0.5-1.0 kg) a week. Over six months that amounts to a weight loss of about 40 lb (18 kg). This concept is more readily understood if the composition of the body of an average women weighing 8 st 9 lb (55 kg) is recalled. Five stone four pounds (34 kg) of her weight consists of water and minerals. Protein accounts for 15 lb (7 kg), and this makes up her muscles and is intimately connected with her vital organs, so that even in advanced starvation (as in severe anorexia nervosa) very little is available to be converted into energy. Less than 2 lb (1 kg) of her weight is due to carbohydrate, but her fatty tissues weigh 24 lb (11 kg). This fat is available for energy needs and if burned up completely will make available about 354 MJ (85 000 kcals) of the 416 MJ (99 000 kcals) contained in her adipose tissues. (The difference is due to the fact that the metabolic process which releases the fat requires energy so the amount available is less than the amount stored in the fatty tissues.)

Case history: Beryl

Beryl is an obese, middle-aged woman, whose height is 5 ft 3 in (1.60 m) and who weighs 11 st 4 lb (72 kg). She is about 2 st 9 lb (17 kg) over-weight, and most of this excess is due to fat she has made and stored over the years when she has eaten more energy in the form of food than she has used up. Beryl has read articles and is worried about being too fat. She would like to get back to her ideal weight of 8 st 9 lb (55 kg). Each day she probably requires to expend about 2000 calories of energy to meet the demands of her body and her work in the house. If she could manage to eat only 1000 calories a day, it would take 125 days – over four months – before she exhausted her stored energy by burning up the fat she had laid down over the years. A diet of only 1000 calories a day is very difficult to stick to, so it is more likely that she would choose a diet which provided 1500 calories a day. On this diet, if she sticks to it exactly, she would burn up 500 calories of stored energy each day and it would take her 250 days – over eight months – for her weight to fall to the ideal! Beryl has a real problem, for it is stupid to pretend that it is easy to lose 2 st 9 lb (17 kg) of weight and it is unlikely, whatever diet she decides upon, that she will manage to do it in less than eight months. As well as this, previously fat people who have managed to reduce their weight by dieting regain weight very quickly, compared with untreated fat people, if they start over-eating again. For this reason, Beryl will have to exert very great will-power to achieve her weight loss and to keep to her lower weight.

The motivation to keep to the chosen reducing diet is increased if the person if aware that even when she keeps to her diet rigorously, her weight may fluctuate within 2–4 lb (1–2 kg). For this reason she should avoid weighing herself more frequently than once a week. It is also important that the diet chosen permits the person to enjoy a social life. It is pointless and counterproductive to be a thinning, antisocial, crotchety recluse – it is better to be fat and enjoy life. Becoming thin should not be made a punishment, nor should an obese person be filled with guilt as well as fat. The diet recommended in this book (and other sensible diets) enable a person to eat with the family and to socialize with friends.

Eating disorders – the facts

There are several other behavioural changes, some of which a person who is dieting may choose to adopt.

However, if any of them makes the person think continually about food it may hinder rather than help her keep to her diet. This applies especially to obese people who binge-eat. For this reason, care should be taken to choose those changes which can be adopted comfortably. They can be listed as follows.

● When on your diet take more exercise – if you enjoy it. Don't exercise and hate it. You will compensate for your dislike by over-eating.

It is helpful if you go for a walk, or do something active, after a meal. There is evidence that this helps you lose weight rather more quickly than if you slump down in front of the television set as soon as you have finished eating. This is because exercise induces heat production and energy loss.

● Don't go on a 'crash diet' which provides less than 500 calories a day. Initially these diets produce a more rapid weight loss, but after a while you will find you cannot keep to the diet, and when you stop you usually overeat. Oddly enough it has been found that on a crash diet you burn up lean body tissue (mostly protein) rather than fat – in fact you burn up no more of your fat stores on a 'crash diet' over a two-month period than if you chose and stick to a 1000 calorie diet.

Crash diets and crazy diets do not really help, despite what the magazines and your friends say. For a short while they seem to succeed, but sooner, rather than later, you find you cannot keep to the diet and you overeat. Back comes the fat – and you become discouraged!

● Choose a diet which is nutritious, and which is sufficiently varied and tasty to enable you to stick to it without getting bored or frustrated. As far as weight loss is concerned it does not matter too much what proportions of carbohydrates, protein, and fat you eat in your diet, so long as it is a low-calorie diet, and so long as it contains sufficient vitamins, minerals, and dietary fibre ('roughage') to keep you in good health. But make each meal attractive to look at, pleasant to smell, and good to taste, so that you learn to enjoy your diet.

● If you limit the dietary fibre in your food you may become constipated and be at risk of other unpleasant disorders. The remedy is

132

easy: eat wholemeal bread in your ration or one or more of the fibre-rich foods mentioned earlier. Dietary fibre will not add to your carbo-hydrate or calorie intake, and it will help you to avoid the side-effects of a 'refined carbohydrate' diet.

● Don't gorge by eating only one large meal a day. You will lose weight more quickly if you eat several small meals spread out over the day — and you will feel more normal if you do this. Do not miss breakfast and do not eat your last meal late at night. The reason for eating several small meals rather than a single large meal is that smaller meals eaten at shorter intervals induce a greater production of body heat, which is then dissipated into the surrounding air. Body heat is pro-duced by using energy, and that is what you are trying to do — to use more energy than you ingest.

● Do try and eat your meals at approximately the same time each day. This has the psychological effect of helping you to control your feelings of hunger at times other than meal times.

● When you have a meal, eat slowly. When you have put food in your mouth do not add any more until your mouth is empty. If it helps, put down your knife, fork, or spoon while your mouth has food in it. And chew your food slowly so that you learn to taste and smell the food to the fullest extent. Psychologists believe that eating slowly and chewing meticulously teaches you to be satisfied with less food and to enjoy the smaller quantity more. Additional dietary fibre will also help you to achieve this objective.

● Every fifteen mouthfuls, stop and put down your eating utensils for about half a minute. This strategy helps you to enjoy more the smaller amount of food you are permitted.

● Before you start eating, decide how much of which food you are going to put on your plate, and do not add more. Once you start eating it is too easy to say to yourself, 'I'll just have a little more'. You must not. 'Littles' add up to a lot and you will not control your eating. It often helps if you put your food on a smaller plate, so that the plate looks fuller! This will help you make do with less.

● As soon as you feel full, stop eating, no matter how much is still on your plate. Indeed, it may help you always to leave some food on your plate, and so break the habit of continuing to eat until all the food on your plate has gone, whether you need it or not.

- Once you feel full or finish your meal, leave the table (if you can do so without offending anybody). Staying at the table where there is food may break your resolve not to eat any more.
- Don't keep packets of sweets, biscuits, chocolate, or nuts in the house or office. If you get bored or unhappy you will be tempted to have a nibble. If they are not there you can resist the temptation. If they are, you will be able to resist everything except the temptation.
- Only go shopping for food when you have eaten. If you do your own shopping, or shop for the family, you may be tempted when you see the delicious-looking foods in the shops. You can resist the temptation to buy and eat these foods if you do three simple things. First, only go shopping after you have eaten. People react less to the sight of food when they are not hungry. Secondly, make out a list of foods you really need before you go shopping. Stick to the list. Do not be tempted by other foods. Thirdly, when possible, only buy foods which need more preparation than just opening the container. This will reduce the risk that you will 'just open a tin or a packet for a little snack'.
- Don't be 'conned' into choosing a complicated or expensive diet. You will not keep to it. Diets which insist that you only eat certain foods on certain days, and other foods only at certain times of the day, should be avoided. They are rubbish. Choose a diet which is no more expensive than your usual food. If you do not, someone will complain and you will become discouraged and stop eating your diet.

Drugs

Although the use of anorectic drugs and of thyroid hormone has been enthusiastically promoted in the treatment of obesity, their value is limited.

Anorectic drugs reduce hunger or increase a feeling of fullness (satiety), but most obese people do not eat because of hunger. Nevertheless, carefully designed studies have shown that patients taking a low energy diet and anorectic medications lose more weight than those on a diet alone, but the effect diminishes or is reversed after about 12 weeks. And when the anorectic drug is stopped, weight is rapidly gained. The place of anorectic drugs in the treatment of obesity is limited, and, at best, they help the patient to come to terms with the need to lose weight over a long period by increasing her morale. In fact,

Obesity

a study of the opinions of 1362 patients about the use of anorectic drugs showed that most preferred diet alone to diet and anorectic drugs. A minority of patients feel that anorectic drugs help. They may take the drugs intermittently over a period of 12 to 14 months, but no course of treatment should exceed 12 weeks. Anorectic drugs may achieve their effect by suggestion rather than by a direct action on the 'satiety' centre in the brain. This is suggested by an investigation which demonstrated that inert injections given to a group of patients produced a greater weight loss than that achieved by most active anti-obesity drugs.

Although thyroid extract is still popular among some doctors for the treatment of obesity, there is little evidence that it is of any value. The use of thyroid extract is based on the belief that people who are morbidly obese lack thyroid hormone. The inference from this belief is that thyroid tablets will help weight reduction. Thyroid tablets are available in two forms: thyroxine and triiodothyronine. Thyroxine, and particularly the more active triiodothyronine, increases the metabolic rate to some extent in people who have no thyroid disorders, but the dose of the thyroid hormone required to produce any significant weight loss causes toxic symptoms in most cases. As well, the weight loss is mainly of lean tissue, not fat. In a careful study of the value of thyroxine in the treatment of obesity, no significant benefit was found over diet alone. Unless the obese person is hypothyroid, thyroid hormones should not be prescribed to increase weight loss.

Clearly, if dietary measures and supportive psychotherapy enable the obese person to lose weight and to maintain the body weight at the desirable level, operations to help achieve weight reduction are unnecessary. It seems however that although almost any fat person can lose weight, few can keep it off. Many reports showing that a particular method was successful are methodologically unsound and have too short a follow-up. It has been demonstrated that most people who achieve an initial weight loss fail to maintain the lower weight for longer than 6 to 12 months. If the study terminates before 12 months, an inaccurate success rate will be reported. In longer-term studies made over 20 years ago, it was noted that few participants lost as much as 16 st (10 kg) and most who did regained weight shortly after treatment ended. A decade later, a large study in Britain showed that

135

between 10 and 40 per cent of participants had lost some weight by the end of the first year of treatment, but fewer than 10 per cent maintained the weight loss for a period of years.

Modern approaches to the problem are first to achieve the weight loss and secondly, to maintain the lower weight by reinforcing the resolve of the person through periodic intervention in the form of supportive psychotherapy. These methods promise a more successful outcome. For example a study of over 700 women who had reduced their weight over an average period of 30 weeks using the Weight Watchers programme, so that it fell to within the 'desirable range' and who continued to attend group meetings periodically, showed that 15 months after the weight loss had been achieved only 30 per cent of the women weighed more than 10 per cent above their 'desirable' weight.

The greater the obesity, the more difficult it is to lose weight permanently; for this reason when non-surgical methods fail, surgical methods, in spite of their dangers may be appropriate.

An obese patient will only achieve and maintain weight reduction if she is motivated, persistent, and prepared to alter her life-style. If she is not prepared to fulfil these conditions, there is little point in persisting with a weight reduction diet. The psychological assessment of an obese patient is an important diagnostic investigation. Many physicians believe that a full psychological evaluation by a clinical psychologist is necessary, but from our discussions with our colleagues, and in our own experience, an assessment based on the questions asked in Chapter 5 may be sufficient.

Jaw-wiring

Those patients who fail to lose a significant amount of weight in spite of keeping to the 4.20 to 5.0 MJ (1000–1200 kcal) diet over a period of weeks or months, or who have an adverse social environment, may choose to have a surgical procedure which may protect them from eating more than their allowance. One such procedure is jaw-wiring. The molar teeth are wired, permitting the jaws to open only about half an inch (1.5 cm) (Fig. 18). This reduces the ability of the person to eat food, unless she removes the wire, homogenizes the food, or 'stuffs' food through the teeth. The person who has had her jaws wired is able to talk easily, but it will be obvious to her friends and relations

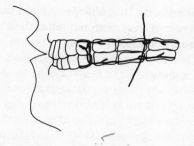

Fig. 18. The technique of jaw wiring.

that her mouth is relatively rigid when she speaks.

Before the molar teeth are wired, the patient has to agree (1) to attend her doctor at four-week intervals for evaluation; (2) to keep the jaws wired until the weight loss is such that no further medical reason for weight loss persists and; (3) to continue dieting when the wires are removed. The reason for the last condition is that binge-eating is likely to occur after removal of the wires with consequent rapid weight gain. The Nutritional Research Group in Britain suggest a device to help the patient conform to the third condition. On the day the wires are removed, a nylon cord is tied around the person's waist! If weight loss is maintained the cord is comfortable, but if more than 13 lb (6 kg) of weight is regained, it becomes uncomfortably tight.

Jaw-wiring can only be done if the person has no psychiatric illness, has healthy teeth and gums, and has a resting metabolic rate which is normal or high: a resting oxygen consumption of less than 240 ml/minute is a contraindication to jaw wiring.

Jaw-wiring is relatively painless, although some discomfort may be felt in the first 24 hours after the procedure. This occurs from spasm of the jaw muscles, from bruising of the gums, or from toothache due to the sideways force on the teeth. Mild sedatives or valium may be required. A few patients develop ulceration of the inside of the cheek or the tongue from movement of the ends of the wires in the first few days after its application. This is easily corrected.

The jaws should not be wired for more than nine months as periodontal problems increase after this time. During the period the jaws are wired, the patient should be seen regularly by a dentist.

Eating disorders – the facts

It may have become clear from this description that the purpose of jaw-wiring is similar to that of admission to hospital in anorexia nervosa. It is to control the person's eating and other weight-related behaviour until she has learned and can accept a new pattern of eating. From this it follows that although the procedure of jaw-wiring is simple, and physical complications are few, psychological problems may occur. The knowledge that the mouth cannot be opened may cause the person to feel a 'prisoner of her weight', and be attended by depression, or by a lack of ability to relate to her partner or family, particularly during the initial weeks after jaw-wiring. To cope with problems during this period, the patient needs moral and physical support from her partner and/or her family, and may be helped further with supportive psychotherapy.

As a steady, relentless weight gain seems inevitable after the wires have been removed, psychotherapy during this period may be helpful, as may the use of the waistcord, but some people with morbid obesity may instead choose a major surgical operation to enable them to alter their disordered eating behaviour.

Major surgical procedures for the treatment of morbid obesity

The majority of people with morbid obesity will lose weight on a strict low-energy diet, supplemented if necessary by jaw-wiring. Many find it difficult to maintain their lower weight once the psychological support they received during weight loss is withdrawn, and within four to eight months many will have regained 50 per cent more of the weight they lost. These rather discouraging results induced physicians interested in treating obesity to review the physiology of digestion and to talk with their surgical colleagues.

The physiology of digestion

The primary function of the digestive tract is to provide the body with a continual supply of water, electrolytes, and nutrients. This is achieved by the movement of the food through the oesophagus, stomach, and intestines; by the secretion of digestive juices; and by the absorption of the digested foods, water, and electrolytes from the intestines.

The movement and mixing of foods occurs because slowly moving peristaltic waves of contractions pass regularly along the alimentary

138

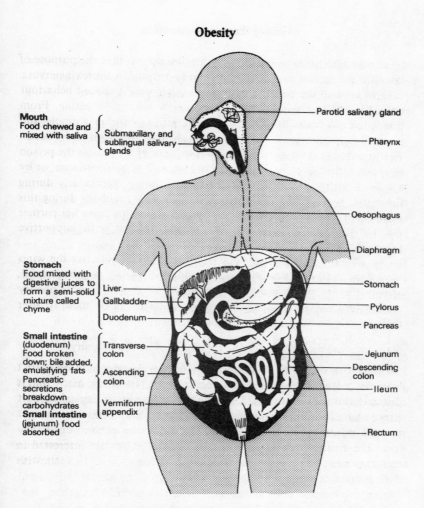

Mouth
Food chewed and
mixed with saliva

Submaxillary and
sublingual salivary
glands

Parotid salivary gland

Pharynx

Oesophagus

Diaphragm

Stomach
Food mixed with
digestive juices to
form a semi-solid
mixture called
chyme

Liver

Gallbladder

Duodenum

Stomach

Pylorus

Pancreas

Small intestine
(duodenum)
Food broken
down; bile added,
emulsifying fats
Pancreatic
secretions
breakdown
carbohydrates
Small intestine
(jejunum) food
absorbed

Transverse
colon

Ascending
colon

Vermiform
appendix

Jejunum

Descending
colon

Ileum

Rectum

Fig. 19. The intestinal tract.

tract in response to its distension by food or water. These contractions
squeeze the food onwards, mixing it at the same time.

In the mouth, food is masticated and mixed with saliva. It is then
swallowed and passes through the oesophagus to enter the stomach.
The stomach can store large quantities of food until it can be accommo-
dated in the intestine. During its period in the stomach the food is

mixed with gastric digestive juices and dilute hydrochloric acid to form a semi-fluid mixture and is partially broken down. As space becomes available in the intestines, the mixture, called chyme, is moved from the stomach by peristaltic waves of contractions.

Most of the absorption of food takes place in the small intestine, where the chyme is acted on by secretions from the pancreas and by intestinal digestive juices. Carbohydrates are further broken down by the pancreatic secretions, and are absorbed, mainly in the jejunum. Fats are emulsified by the action of bile salts and digested by secretions from the pancreas and intestines to form free fatty acids, monoglycerides, and glycerol. In this state they are absorbed by the intestines, and the greater the distension of the intestines, the greater is the absorption. Protein is further broken down in the intestines into its constituent amino acids and absorbed. It is clear from these observations that most of the absorption of food takes place in the small intestine.

Understanding of these physiological concepts led to the idea that if most of the jejunum was by-passed by cutting it near its junction with the duodenum and anastomosing the cut end to the lower part of the ileum, the patient would be able to eat what she liked but would lose weight, because the food would be neither digested nor absorbed. A second idea, which was developed somewhat later, as the complications following jejuno-ileal bypass surgery became apparent, was to reduce the size of the stomach. It was argued that if the size of the stomach was reduced by two-thirds, or more, the patient would be prevented from eating large meals because a feeling of fullness (or satiety) would rapidly come over her when she ate.

The effect of surgery, either jejunoileal bypass or gastric reduction, is to reduce considerably the amount of energy absorbed, enabling the patient to lose weight steadily and to reach her 'desirable' weight after 6–15 months. It is also expected that the limited amount of food eaten, or energy absorbed, will enable the person to maintain her desired weight, once she had achieved it, and her weight will not increase.

Jejuno-ileal bypass

Jejuno-ileal bypass was first performed in the 1950s. The operation became popular in the early 1970s, and has now been performed over

10 000 times, mainly in the USA. The operation has been modified since its first introduction, as undesirable side-effects became apparent. The earlier versions, in which the first 14 in (35 cm) of the jejunum was anastomosed to the last 4 in (10 cm) of the ileum, were followed by severe metabolic side-effects (Fig. 20). Fat was not absorbed (which

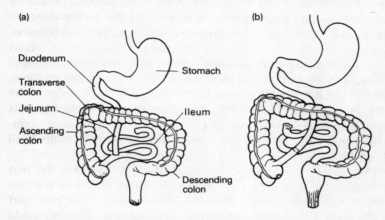

Fig. 20. (a) The end-to-side jejunoileal shunt of Payne; (b) the end-to-end jejunoileal shunt of Scott.

was the main purpose of the operation), but remained in the bowel where it broke down and prevented the absorption of the fat-soluble vitamins A and D. The breakdown products of fat formed insoluble soaps with calcium and magnesium, which increased the retention of water in the bowel leading to diarrhoea and to steatorrhoea. The frequency of bowel movements, and the chemical nature of the faeces, caused inflammation of the rectum in about one-third to one-half of patients, and to an increased incidence of haemorrhoids. In the normal gut, calcium is bound to oxalate, but after jejuno-ileal by-pass the oxalate becomes free and may be absorbed, leading to oxalate stones in the kidneys. Further, as other high energy substances in the diet, particularly carbohydrate, are also poorly absorbed, they are fermented by the bacteria in the gut leading to bloating, and the formation of gas which is expelled either by belching or as flatus.

The side-effects are due to the fact that the food is neither digested nor absorbed in the shortened small intestine. It was originally thought that the lack of absorption of energy was the main reason for the observed weight loss after by-pass surgery. However, there is now evidence that malabsorption reduces energy intake considerably and that the major factor in the loss of weight is that the patient eats considerably less after the operation. The anorexia occurs because overeating makes the patient feel ill. He becomes bloated easily, passes foul smelling flatus, and tends to have irritating fluid stools.

In addition, bypass surgery alters zinc and copper levels in the blood and reduces the secretion of various hormones and enzymes which are involved in the absorption and assimilation of food. It is speculated that these alterations may cause the brain to recognize a state of satiety earlier, so that the person eats less.

The long-term complications which follow jejuno-ileal bypass are so severe in many cases that the operation is coming under increasing critical scrutiny. A computerized search of all publications between 1963 and 1977, found 171 references to complications in accounts dealing with a total of 6319 patients. Unfortunately, for analysis, many of the reports were poorly written, omitted important data, and had an insufficiently long follow-up. In addition, there was a lack of control groups. However, the study showed that the death rate following operation was 2.8 per cent, and one-fifth of the people died within one month of surgery. Long-term complications were poorly reported in many publications, but a study of selected reports dealing with 50 or more patients showed that they were not uncommon (Table 8).

Case history: Ken

I often sit and think back, was it worth all the problems I have been through.

It all started in 1969 when I asked for a new uniform as I was too fat for the old one, and I was told that I would have to lose weight, because there was not a wardsman's uniform in any larger size than what I already had.

So the next step was to see the staff doctor for a referral to a physician, who suggested that I attend a psychiatrist for hypnosis. I talked to my wife about this, and she suggested that I see a dietitian rather than a psychiatrist.

I did this but had no willpower to stick to a diet, because the slightest

Table 8. *Complications and undesirable side-effects after jejunoileal by-pass surgery*

	Per cent of patients developing complications
Wound complications	15–25
Severe metabolic (mineral) disturbances	20–30
Ano-rectal pain/discomfort	35–50
Haemorrhoids	14–20
Severe (offensive) diarrhoea	15–20
Bloating, wind, flatus	10–15
Arthritis	8–12
Kidney stones	8–12
Gall-stones	3–7
Psychiatric problems	6–10
Liver failure	3–5
Death	0.5–4
Re-operation required	10–20

Follow-up 3 years, often only 1 year

upset would make me eat and eat. So eventually I went along to the psychiatrist. But after a couple of visits, I was not too impressed and decided to go and try something else.

My physician was involved with jejuno-ileal by-pass operations to lose weight and thought that this might be the answer to my problems, but I should first try dieting.

He weighed me in at 20½ stone (130 kg) and took pulse, blood pressure and temperature readings and all the normal things, and then asked the questions about my past. I explained that at a young age I was not overweight, it was in my mid-teens that the weight started to build up. I took his advice and tried different diets but could not stick to them, and then I had a nasty experience.

I was walking up the hallway of my house and I collapsed. I was taken to the hospital and the doctor there said that I had had a blood pressure attack, and that either I took the weight off within 6 months or I would have 6 months to live. At that stage I was 22 stone (140 kg). I went on a 500 calorie a day diet, and I was taking Duramine M40 tablets. I was also going to a doctor every second day and having female hormone injections, called chorionic gonadotrophin, which he said would guarantee I would lose weight.

143

In 5 months I lost 9 stone (57 kg). I kept this off for four years until late 1973, and then with my wife expecting our youngest son, and I was in threat of being retrenched from my job, I put all the weight back on again in 7 months, up again to 20 stone (109 kg).

After I had explained all this to my doctor, he told me about the operation in detail. He explained that the surgeon would by-pass the small intestine leaving about 20 inches (50 cm) but the remainder of the intestine would stay inside me.

Then he proceeded to tell me the side effects such as diarrhoea, which would mean opening my bowels about five times a day, and that I might have wind pains and also a strict diet to stick to.

This sounded too good to be true, it was like waving a lollipop in front of a baby. So I agreed to the operation, and things went into action.

A date was arranged, and I went into hospital ten days before the operation was due to be performed. I underwent a lot of tests, such as: one day they would make me go without food, and the next day they would take core samples of fatty tissues from my buttocks. Then the next day they would give me really fatty foods such as milkshakes made of cream and radioactive fatty oil or something like that, and the next day the core tests would be done again.

Then came the operation. About 4 hours later I was back in bed, my wife was there and so were my doctors. I was, of course, very dopey.

In the next few days I went through a lot of pain, I was suffering a lot of cramps and wind pains, I also had a lot of vomiting, and as a result I was only allowed to drink a litre of fluid per day. Then the diarrhoea started, and after about 5 days the nurses sat me on the side of the bed, they walked out and left me there. Five minutes later the bed tipped up, and I ended up on the floor wrapped around tubes and things, I could not move until they came back to help me. A doctor came to examine me to see if there was any damage done, and it was discovered that I had busted a tension stitch.

For the next 13 weeks I had a lot of diet and blood problems which were treated in various ways. I was released from hospital when these things were thought to be sorted out.

I was at home for about three weeks and was opening my bowels about 20 times a day, and I was very weak. My wife was suffering because of this, and was run off her feet with looking after me and running after the 3 children, as I could not do anything for her or myself.

I went back to see the physician and he had blood tests done and it was found that I had a low blood potassium. This was treated by admitting me to hospital and using a drip.

About 3 months after that, I was suffering a lot of abdominal pain, so I went back to him and he said I had an incisional hernia. I was admitted to hospital again and I had it repaired. I watched the operation as I had an epidural block, because I had such a bad reaction to anaesthetics.

Both of these problems (blood and hernia) repeated themselves; the hernia twice and different sorts of blood problems repeated themselves on numerous occasions, and were treated the same way, by admission to hospital. It seemed never ending the weeks in hospital away from my wife and kids over a period of about four years.

I then started to go to a new family doctor, and after a period of time he discovered that I had a magnesium deficiency, so this was also treated. I went back again to the physician, and he noticed that I had a lot of muscle wastage on my left side, and I had practically no strength and was extremely weak. He said it was congenital, but my father said that I was a normal child. It was proved later that I had spinal nerve damage. I have a lot of muscle wastage on my left side and sometimes my leg collapses from under me. This happened on one occasion and I fell and broke my right hip, which meant another operation to put a pin and plate in my hip, this was removed in September of this year 1982, three years after it happened.

From the constant diarrhoea, I have had about 5 fissure operations on my back passage; this happens about every 12 to 18 months.

All this has caused me to be off work for, so far, 8 years, and as far as I can see, no end to it all.

My weight now fluctuates between 12 and 12½ stone (76–79 kg). In the mornings I have a pretty normal flat tummy, but as the day goes on I blow up in the tummy like a balloon, as a result of this I have to have two sets of clothes, one set for the morning and another set for the afternoon to night time.

I have a blood test once a month and two injections once a month as well as vitamin B_{12} injection and a vitamin K injection. If I happen to be a few days overdue for these injections my muscles ache and I become pale and weak.

The operation has been successful as far as my losing weight is concerned, but if I had my way again, I would try something else as the emotional strain on myself and my family has left a lot of scars.

In another study (made in 1979) of 101 patients treated by jejuno-ileal bypass between 1972 and 1975, 28 were dead. Of the remaining 73, 70 were available for follow-up. Twenty-one per cent of them had no problems, 34 per cent had minor problems, and the remaining 45 per cent had major problems. Moreover, one-third of the patients had regained their former weight. The authors concluded 'the use of jejuno-ileal bypass as a means of weight reduction appears to be unjustified, particularly in view of the frequent inadequate loss of weight'.

An even more critical evaluation of jejuno-ileal bypass was made by another surgeon in 1980. In a randomized trial he compared his own series of jejuno-ileal bypass with gastric bypass. The study led him to abandon jejuno-ileal bypass for medical and ethical reasons:

Jejuno-ileal bypass is no longer an acceptable or defensible operation because of the prohibitive morbidity — liver failure, malnutrition, enteritis, oxalate urinary tract stones, arthritis and osteomalacia — and the expense related to post-operative outpatient and inpatient care, long-term follow-up, and the symptoms, caused by the diarrhoea that seriously interfere with the quality of the patient's life. Gastric bypass by comparison is associated with low morbidity, minimal postoperative medical expense, and a high quality of life. The early experience with gastroplasty indicates this may be a better operation. It should be safer than gastric bypass since no anastomosis is performed. In concluding an important message that I want to transmit is that the surgeon who performs jejuno-ileal bypass has the responsibility to insure adequate follow-up of his patients for the duration of their lives.

The present consensus of opinion regarding jejuno-ileal bypass was expressed in 1981 in an editorial in the *Journal of the American Medical Association* which stated bluntly, 'In a current assessment of obesity management, one is compelled to reject jejuno-ileal bypass as a metabolically and physiologically unsafe procedure.'

Gastric bypass and gastric reduction

Gastric bypass and gastric reduction as methods of reducing energy intake have been less popular than jejuno-ileal bypass as earlier researchers found that the loss of weight was less. The initial suggestion was to reduce the size of the stomach by cutting it and to anastomize its upper portion with the jejunum. Most experience has been with this procedure (Fig. 21). More recently gastric stapling has been adopted (Fig. 22). This effectively reduces the size of the stomach leaving a small aperture between the upper portion (the volume of which is about 50 ml) and the lower larger portion. The size of the aperture is maintained by using 'hemstitch' of unabsorbable material (Prolene). The size of the aperture appears crucial to the long-term success of the operation. The effect of gastric 'partitioning' is that the person feels 'full' and uncomfortable after eating a small amount of food, because the small pouch is stretched and messages are sent to the 'satiety centre'

146

Obesity

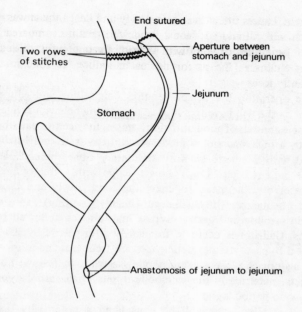

Fig. 21. Gastric bypass.

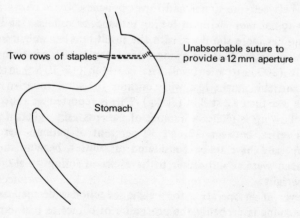

Fig. 22. Gastric stapling.

in the brain. Unless the patient eats slowly and keeps the amount small, the pouch will fill and additional food will remain in the oesophagus, leading to heartburn or vomiting. As both are uncomfortable, as is the feeling of 'fullness', the patient learns to reduce his food intake and consequently loses weight.

Before operation the person requires counselling and education in nutrition, as she will have to adopt to new eating behaviour. She will be taught the essentials of good nutrition, that is, the need to eat a balanced diet, with a high protein, a moderate carbohydrate and low-fat content, and with adequate amounts of dietary fibre, minerals, and vitamins; the patient is also taught how to cope with a greatly diminished gastric reservoir, the need to chew the food slowly and thoroughly and the consequences which will occur (mainly vomiting) if she does not.

Gastric stapling and gastric bypass may also be followed by complications. Gall-stones occur as frequently after gastric bypass as after jejuno-ileal bypass, vitamin deficiences are frequent, and a few patients develop a stomach ulcer. Gastric stapling seems to be followed by fewer side-effects, particularly the metabolic upsets, than gastric bypass, but the follow-up period is short.

Gastric stapling must still be considered a potentially dangerous operation. The staples may separate, leading to leakage in the first days a week after operation; the size of the pouch may increase, as may the opening between the upper and lower pouches. These changes enable a person to eat more without feeling satiated, or vomiting, and as soon as she can eat more she does, with the result that her weight increases. There is no doubt that following gastric stapling (or gastric bypass) a 31 st 6 lb (200 kg) patient will lose 26–44 lb (12–20 kg) in the first month, and the weight loss will continue for some months until the weight is less than 12 st 8 lb (80 kg). This is reported as a success, but if the follow-up is longer a number of patients gain weight. In several reported series, between 20 and 30 per cent of patients were lost to follow-up, and have to be considered as failures, because those who were traced were found either to have ceased losing weight or to be gaining weight.

However, if an operation for weight reduction is deemed necessary, gastric stapling is probably the procedure of choice as it is as effective in reducing weight as the jejuno-ileal bypass operation; it is followed by one-third the 'rehospitalization rate' and few long-term complications develop. The patient must clearly understand, before operation, that the creation of a small pouch during an operation which may last 1½ to 2 hours, will not cure a lifetime's addiction to food or alter disordered eating habits. The patient must also be aware that following operation, vitamin and mineral supplements are necessary, pain may occur, as may episodes of diarrhoea; and appropriate follow-up including blood tests is essential.

Case history: Gareth

I was always pretty big and when I was 16 I played Rugby League. Then I weighed about 15 stone (89 kg), but it was all muscle – no fat. That's when I started working in the blast furnace. I drank like a fish and ate like a horse but worked it out and sweated it out so I didn't put on any weight in that job. I didn't like the job much and so I got this job with the railways. The problem was that in the new job I just sat down for 8–10 hours a day and mostly did nothing, but I still had the same eating and drinking habits. So I started putting on weight and got up to 24 stone (153 kg). I was so fat I found it hard to do my job. The railways doctor said I'd have to lose weight or he'd take me off driving. I tried diets, weight watchers and all the rest, but it didn't do any good. When you work shifts there's no way you can keep to a diet. I drank a lot of coffee and when you have coffee you have to have biscuits or a sandwich. Then I tried exercise. That didn't work either. I'd play football and then go to the pub. Playing made me hungry. So I ate more. And here I was, 24 stone (153 kg) and getting fatter.

About this time I read about some operations and experiments they were doing in the States, someone was telling me about it where they put a plastic tube inside your intestines so that the wall couldn't absorb the food as it was blocked off. So I went and saw my doctor about it and straight out he said 'I don't agree with it. You are over-weight but you have a big frame. You are a big boned boy and you can carry that weight with no trouble. As far as I am concerned, if you can't lose the weight on a diet you're going to have to put up with it.' Then I was over at another doctor and she started asking me about my weight. I told her I had asked my doctor about it and she said 'Oh, go and see this bloke' and sent me off to my surgeon.

He told me about the two types of operations he was doing at the time, one that he was doing before where he stitched across the stomach and took a piece of the bowel out and rerouted it into the top

149

of the stomach. He also told me about this other one that he eventually did on me. And that was to make my stomach smaller by stapling across it. He called it gastric partitioning.

He did the operation one Wednesday. I didn't feel too bad after it, I was doped up to my ears the first couple of days with painkillers and felt nothing. Bill – that's my surgeon – is one of these blokes who are sticklers for exercise and I was up walking around the second day though the walk was more like a slow crawl. He told me I wouldn't want to eat much because I would feel full quickly. When I was in hospital and did start eating again it was on a puree diet, everything blended and only in very small amounts. When I came home I stayed on the puree for a while then gradually started experimenting around with what I could take and what I couldn't. Before I had the operation I would eat a 2 lb rump steak and have a couple of beers and a bottle of wine. But I couldn't do that after the operation. I felt full quickly and if I didn't chew the food into small pieces, up it would come. It couldn't get through the hole or something. Bill had told me that before the operation. He told me what I would be able to eat but that everything would have to be chewed thoroughly until it was pulp because it had to go through the hole of about $\frac{1}{8}$ or $\frac{1}{4}$ of an inch. If you don't chew it enough to let it go through there it comes back. So I adjusted my eating habits. I ate less and chewed well. I still get some regurgitation but not much. I think I'm a hell of a lot fitter than I was before and I think that because I carried the weight for so long I'm a lot fitter than many other blokes. For example, I suppose about 12 months after the operation I went along to the beach to do a bit of jogging to see how far I could go. I used to be able to jog a mile, no worries, when I was overweight. Well, I went from one end of the beach to the other and back and three quarters of the way back again, which would probably be nearer 4 or 5 miles and I wasn't even puffing at the end of it, no strain, no nothing, just felt like a walk across the road.

The operation made me change how much I ate and how I ate. It also stopped me drinking beer. Wine is OK, but the gas in beer blows your stomach up and it hurts.

I had a problem about two years after the operation. It seems the hole had got narrower and I couldn't keep anything down – even water. So I saw Bill, and he said 'Back to hospital, over you go'. They put a gastric tube down and pumped my stomach out, put a drip in to feed me and I stayed there for 3 days. They put a thing down to have a look, couldn't see anything and Bill said 'We'll have to open you up and find out what is wrong'. So he opened it up, fixed it and found I had a few gallstones so he took the gall bladder while he was there, and since that I've been well. I'm down to 12 stone (70 kg). I can go out and eat a meal. I don't each much red meat and I'm off steaks because

150

Obesity

Table 9. *The appropriate management of morbid obesity*

Appropriate	Inappropriate
Low-energy, nutritionally balanced diet for > 6 months	Complex crazy fad diets
Moderate regular exercise	Excessive exercise with dieting
	Sauna baths
	Electric treatment
Supportive psychotherapy	
? Anorectic drugs (short term less than 4 months)	Diuretics
	Thyroid hormones
Surgery	
? Jaw-wiring	Jejuno-ileal bypass
Gastric reduction	

by the time you've cut it up small and chewed it, the rest is cold. I'm enjoying life. But it is good to know that I can contact Bill if anything goes wrong.

Would I have had the operation if I'd known what it meant? Thinking back I would, but when I came out of surgery and for a couple of weeks after that and the two lots of surgery I've had, up until 6 months ago I doubted whether I would. One of the blokes at work has just been recommended to have it done and he asked me if I would recommend it. I said 'No, I wouldn't recommend it but if you want it, have it, it helped me.'

THE PHYSICAL AND PSYCHOLOGICAL BENEFITS OF WEIGHT REDUCTION IN GROSS OBESITY

In spite of the dangers of operations for gross obesity, in spite of complications which may follow surgery; in spite of the need for careful attention to diet, in spite of the need for vitamin and mineral supplements, and the need for frequent visits for 'follow-up', the choice must ultimately be that of the patient. There is no doubt of the physical benefits of weight reduction. Cardiac function improves and the level of the blood pressure is reduced, which reduces the risk of a stroke. The blood circulation to the legs improves with a reduction in thrombophlebitis. There is an improvement in pulmonary ventilation, with a reduction in shortness of breath. If the person has osteoarthritis, or low

151

back pain, the severity of the pain is reduced. Following a significant reduction in weight there is an increase in energy and a reduction in fatigue.

The psychological benefits of surgical measures to achieve weight reduction have been less clearly delineated. As weight loss progresses, patients perceive their bodies more favourably and become more self-confident about their personality. The majority of women see themselves as more feminine and more sexually attractive; however, there is no change in the frequency of sexual activity or in sexual pleasure. They experience fewer mood changes and see themselves as more self-assured, outgoing and comfortable. They become more sociable, less preoccupied by weight, and less likely to eat more than they intended at meals or between meals. In spite of these positive findings, many others still feel that they are large, and in psychological tests tend to over-estimate their body size.

These findings suggest that grossly obese people who have failed to reduce their weight significantly by dieting or perhaps jaw-wiring, or fail to maintain the lower weight, may benefit physically and psychologically from surgery, but must weigh up the advantages and disadvantages of the operations.

Obesity

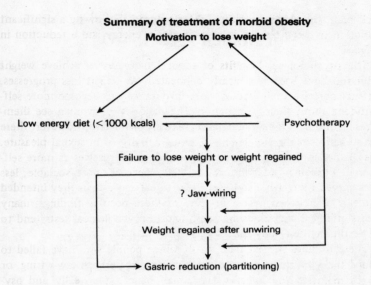

Summary of treatment of morbid obesity
Motivation to lose weight

Low energy diet (< 1000 kcals)   Psychotherapy

Failure to lose weight or weight regained

? Jaw-wiring

Weight regained after unwiring

Gastric reduction (partitioning)

Appendix: Average weight of women aged 15–69

Average weight of women aged 15-69 (standard body weight)

Height (in shoes)		Average weights in pounds and kilograms (in indoor clothing)															
		15–16 years		17–19 years		20–24 years		25–29 years		30–39 years		40–49 years		50–59 years		60–69 years	
ft in	cm	lb	kg	lb	kg	lb	kg	lb	kg	lb	kg	lb	kg	lb	kg	lb	kg
						Women											
4 10	147.3	97	44	99	44.9	102	46.3	107	48.5	115	52.2	122	55.3	125	56.7	127	57.6
4 10½	148.6	98.5	44.7	100.5	45.6	103.5	46.9	108.5	49.2	116	52.6	123	55.8	126	57.2	128	58.1
4 11	149.9	100	45.4	102	46.3	105	47.6	110	49.9	117	53.1	124	56.2	127	57.6	129	58.5
4 11½	151.1	101.5	46	103.5	46.9	106.5	48.3	111.5	50.6	118.5	53.8	125.5	56.9	128.5	58.3	130	59
5 0	152.4	103	46.7	105	47.6	108	49	113	51.3	120	54.4	127	57.6	130	59	131	59.4
5 0½	153.7	105	47.6	107	48.5	110	49.9	114.5	51.9	121.5	55.1	128.5	58.3	131.5	59.6	132.5	60.1
5 1	154.9	107	48.5	109	49.4	112	50.8	116	52.6	123	55.8	130	59	133	60.3	134	60.8
5 1½	156.2	109	49.4	111	50.3	113.5	51.5	117.5	53.3	124.5	56.5	131.5	59.6	134.5	61	135.5	61.5
5 2	157.5	111	50.3	113	51.3	115	52.2	119	54	126	57.2	133	60.3	136	61.7	137	62.1
5 2½	158.8	112.5	51	114.5	51.9	116.5	52.8	120.5	54.7	127.5	57.8	134.5	61	138	62.6	139	63
5 3	160	114	51.7	116	52.6	118	53.5	122	55.3	129	58.5	136	61.7	140	63.5	141	64
5 3½	161.3	115.5	52.4	118	53.5	119.5	54.2	123.5	56	130.5	59.2	138	62.6	142	64.4	143	64.9
5 4	162.6	117	53.1	120	54.4	121	54.9	125	56.7	132	59.9	140	63.5	144	65.3	145	65.8
5 4½	163.8	119	54	122	55.3	123	55.8	127	57.6	133.5	60.6	141.5	64.2	146	66.2	147	66.7
5 5	165.1	121	54.9	124	56.2	125	56.7	129	58.5	135	61.2	143	64.9	148	67.1	149	67.6
5 5½	166.4	123	55.8	125.5	56.9	127	57.6	131	59.4	137	62.1	145	65.8	150	68	151	68.5
5 6	167.6	125	56.7	127	57.6	129	58.5	133	60.3	139	63	147	66.7	152	68.9	153	69.4
5 6½	168.9	126.5	57.4	128.5	58.3	130.5	59.2	134.5	61	140.5	63.7	149	67.6	154	69.9	155	70.3
5 7	170.2	128	58.1	130	59	132	59.9	136	61.7	142	64.4	151	68.5	156	70.8	157	71.2
5 7½	171.5	130	59	132	59.9	134	60.8	138	62.6	144	65.3	153	69.4	158	71.7	159	72.1
5 8	172.7	132	59.9	134	60.8	136	61.7	140	63.5	146	66.2	155	70.3	160	72.6	161	73
5 8½	174	134	60.8	136	61.7	138	62.6	142	64.4	148	67.1	157	71.2	162	73.5	163	73.9
5 9	175.3	136	61.7	138	62.6	140	63.5	144	65.3	150	68	159	72.1	164	74.4	165	74.8
5 9½	176.5	–	–	140	63.5	142	64.4	146	66.2	152	68.9	161.5	73.3	166.5	75.5	–	–
5 10	177.8	–	–	142	64.4	144	65.3	148	67.1	154	69.9	164	74.4	169	76.7	–	–
5 10½	179.1	–	–	144.5	65.5	146.5	66.5	150.5	68.3	156.5	71	166.5	75.5	171.5	77.8	–	–
5 11	180.3	–	–	147	66.7	149	67.6	153	69.4	159	72.1	169	76.7	174	78.9	–	–
5 11½	181.6	–	–	149.5	67.8	151.5	68.7	155.5	70.5	161.5	73.3	171.5	77.8	177	80.3	–	–
6 0	182.9	–	–	152	68.9	154	69.9	158	71.7	164	74.4	174	78.9	180	81.6	–	–

1) Insured persons in the United States. From Society of Actuaries, *Build and Blood Pressure Study*, vol. I, Chicago, 1959, page 16, with interpolations by the editors of these *Scientific Tables*.

The average body weight and percentage deviations used in this book were derived from the above table. Recently the average body weight for height and age has been *increased* both in Great Britain and the USA and new tables are expected. The change does not alter the arguments made here, and further emphasizes that to look fashionably slim most young women diet.

Further reading

Bruch, Hilda. *Eating disorders, obesity, anorexia nervosa and the person within*. Routledge Kegan Paul, London (1974) and *The golden cage*. Open Books, Somerset (1978).

Before writing this book Hilda Bruch had been involved in treatment of people with eating disorders for 40 years. She believes that people develop an eating disorder to avoid having to cope with an aspect of their life. She stresses that treatment must be individual and that the aim is not only to restore normal eating behaviour but to ensure the happiness of the 'person within'.

Crisp, A. *Anorexia nervosa – Let me be*. Academic Press, London (1980).

Crisp's theory is that young women develop anorexia nervosa because they seek to return to being a child biologically and, in many ways socially and psychologically. They fear the challenges of adolescence, with its maturative and sexual connotations.

Dally, P. and Gomez, J. *Obesity and anorexia nervosa – A question of shape*. Faber, London (1980).

This book gives an outline of the problem of eating disorders, and describes the ways in which treatment is undertaken. Written for the general reader it gives much information in a clear concise way.

Palmer, R.L. *Anorexia nervosa – A guide for sufferers and their families*. Penguin, Harmondsworth. (1980).

Trained at St. George' Medical School, Palmer supports Crisp's view that anorexia nervosa is due to a psychobiological regression to childhood. Written for the general reader, the book acquaints sufferers from anorexia nervosa and their families of the possibilities for treatment and of the probable outcomes.

Garfinkle, P.E. and Garner, D.M. *Anorexia nervosa, a multidimensional perspective*. Brunner Mazel, New York (1983).

This is an excellent book, written for health professionals. The extensive literature about anorexia nervosa and anorexia nervosa with bulimia episodes is critically evaluated. The many studies made by the Toronto group are reported and placed in perspective. The book is written in lucid English, and integrates the physiological, psychological, and clinical aspects of a complex, multi-dimensional eating disorder.

Garrow, J.S. *Treat obesity seriously*. Churchill-Livingstone, Edinburgh, (1981).

Dr Garrow has headed a research group into nutritional problems for some years and has written extensively about obesity. This book is designed to help general practitioners and general (fat?) readers understand the biological problems associated with obesity. A personal account, it gives an excellent review of the problems and of treatment strategies.

Glossary

Adipose tissue.	The tissues of the body which contain numbers of fat cells. Adipose tissue is 80 per cent fat, 2 per cent protein, and 18 per cent water. Because of the large proportion of fat, adipose tissue is often called fatty tissue.
Alkalosis.	An increase in the alkalinity of the blood, which normally is slightly acid. It is usually due to an increase in the level of bicarbonate in the blood.
Amenorrhoea.	The cessation or absence of menstruation for more than 3 months
Anastomose.	To join together two hollow tubes; in this case to join the stomach to the intestine.
Anorexia nervosa.	See p. 12 for definition.
Average Body Weight.	The average body weight for age, height, and weight. (The tables are shown in the Appendix, p. 155).
Bariatric physician.	A doctor who specializes in treating obesity.
Bulimia.	See p. 17 for definition.
Biceps.	The muscle extending from the shoulder to the elbow joint, on the front surface of the arm.
Calories.	A lay term for kilocalories (see entry for kilocalories).
Carbohydrates.	The class of nutrients made up of starches and sugars. Carbohydrates provide the main source of energy needed for the human body to function. Starches are the most common form of dietary carbohydrate, and are found in cereal grains, roots, and tubers. In the human gut starches are broken down to sugars, finally to glucose, which is absorbed into the blood.
Chorionic gonadotrophin.	A hormone derived from the placenta which was used to treat obesity. Also known as human chorionic gonadotrophin, or HCG.
Diuretics.	Drugs which act on the kidney to increase the flow of urine.
Electrolytes.	A compound which dissolved in water, separates into electrically charged particles (ions) capable of conducting an electrical current.
Flatus.	'Wind' or gas accumulated in the bowel and expelled through the anus (back passage).

Glossary

Follicle-stimulating hormone.	A hormone secreted by the pituitary gland that stimulates the growth of the egg follicles in the ovary, and the development of sperm in the testis.
Gastroplasty.	An operation on the stomach in which a small section is 'partitioned', so that the size of the stomach is effectively reduced.
Glycogen.	The form in which sugars and starches are stored in animals. Sucrose and starches from plants are converted into glucose before being absorbed into the human body from the gut; and the glucose is converted into glycogen for storage in the liver and in muscle.
Gonadotrophin.	A substance, usually a hormone, capable of stimulating the ovaries or the testicles (trophin means growth).
Gonadotrophic-releasing hormone.	A substance secreted by the hypothalamus which is carried by blood-vessels to the pituitary gland, to stimulate the production and release of the gonadotrophic hormones.
Hypothalamus.	The part of the brain just above the brain-stem which controls the activity of the pituitary gland.
Ketosis.	An accumulation of excessive amounts of chemical compounds in the tissues, which produces acidity in the body tissues and fluids.
Kilojoule.	Measure of energy, which has replaced the K calorie. One kilojoule = 0.24 K calorie.
Kilocalories.	A kilocalorie (also called Kcalories, Kcals, or calories) is a measure of the energy in foods. It is defined as the amount of heat required to raise the temperature of a litre of water from 15 °C to 16 °C. Each food contains a different amount of energy which is absorbed into the body after eating, and expended to keep the body functioning. Recently Kcals have been replaced by a new energy measurement called a kilojoule. 1 Kcal = 4.19 kj.
Lanugo.	Soft, downy hair, similar to that found in small babies.
Laxatives.	Drugs which act on the bowel to increase the speed of the passage of food and of the stools through the gut. They cause soft and frequent motions.
Libido.	A person's sexual desire, arousal, and awareness.
Luteinizing hormone.	A hormone secreted by and released from the pituitary gland which leads to the release of a mature egg (or ovum) from an ovarian follicle, and converts the follicle into a corpus luteum (or yellow body).

159

Eating disorders — the facts

Megajoule.

This is a measure of energy in foods, or expended by the body. 1 megajoule (MJ) = 1000 Kilojoule (KJ) = 239 Kcals.

Menarche.

The onset of menstruation.

Milliliter (ml).

Equivalent to 0.035 fluid ounce.

Obesity.

See p. 21 for defintion.

See p. 21 for defintion.

Osteomalacia.

Thinning of the bones.

Peristalsis.

The wave-like progressive, sequential movement of the wall of the intestines, which churns up food and moves it on towards the anus.

Picking behaviour.

Moving from food in cupboard, to pantry, to fridge to pick and eat small quantities of various foods.

Pituitary gland.

The gland located at the base of the brain, that affects the function of other glands, by releasing special hormones.

Quetelet Index.

A measure devised over 100 years ago to determine whether a person is of normal weight, underweight or obese. The calculation is made in the following way:

$$\frac{\text{Weight in kilograms}}{\text{Height in metres} \times \text{Height in metres}}$$

for example, a woman aged 24 weighs 46 kg and is 1.57 metres tall.

$$46 \div 1.57 \times 1.57 = 18.6$$

The index of 18.6 indicates that she is underweight.

Resistance behaviour.

Behaviour used as methods of stopping abnormal eating patterns.

Satiety (Satiation).

The feeling of 'fullness' after eating food.

Steatorrhoea.

Offensive, loose, 'fatty' stools.

Suprailiac.

The region of the body just above the pelvic bones which identifies a person's waist.

Subscapular.

The area of the body just below the shoulder blades.

Triceps.

The muscle on the back of the upper arm.

Venous thrombosis.

A clot in a vein.

Index

Index